GAY AN
LESBIA
COUPLES

GAY AND LESBIAN COUPLES

Voices from Lasting Relationships

Richard A. Mackey, Bernard A. O'Brien, and Eileen F. Mackey

Westport, Connecticut
London

Library of Congress Cataloging-in-Publication Data

Mackey, Richard A.
    Gay and lesbian couples : voices from lasting relationships /
    Richard A. Mackey, Bernard A. O'Brien, and Eileen F. Mackey.
        p. cm.
    Includes bibliographical references and index.
    ISBN 0–275–95846–9 (alk. paper).—ISBN 0–275–95847–7 (pbk. : alk.
paper)
    1. Gay male couples—United States. 2. Lesbian couples—United
States. 3. Interpersonal relations—United States.
4. Interpersonal communication—United States. 5. Intimacy
(Psychology)—United States. I. O'Brien, Bernard A. II. Mackey,
Eileen F., 1936– . III. Title.
HQ76.3.U5M324 1997
306.76′6—dc21   97–11079

British Library Cataloguing in Publication Data is available.

Library of Congress Catalog Card Number: 97–11079
ISBN: 0–275–95846–9
        0–275–95847–7 (pbk.)

First published in 1997

Praeger Publishers, 88 Post Road West, Westport, CT 06881
An imprint of Greenwood Publishing Group, Inc.

Printed in the United States of America

The paper used in this book complies with the
Permanent Paper Standard issued by the National
Information Standards Organization (Z39.48–1984).

10 9 8 7 6 5 4 3 2 1

For
Cathy and Mary
Greg and John

Contents

Figures

Preface

Until recent years the voices of gays and lesbians were still. Although homosexuality is as old as heterosexuality, relatively little attention has been paid to studying the lifestyles of gay and lesbian couples. One of the more effective ways of neutralizing the social ills of oppression and prejudice directed toward lesbian and gays is through human understanding. In the spirit of furthering the understanding of an important minority group in our society, our work focuses on how individuals in committed relationships adapt to each other as they live out their lives together from the early years of their relationships through the present time. The voices are those of seventy-two individual partners in thirty-six committed, same-sex relationships that have lasted for more than fifteen years.

Our goal in writing the book is to sensitize people, regardless of their sexual orientations, to the world of lasting relationships of lesbian and gay couples. This book breaks new ground in exploring the development of relationships among couples about whom relatively little is known. It speaks to the need for seeing others clearly rather than through a stereotypical lens.

As social scientists we are committed to understanding the human condition in its many forms and shapes. Understanding without judgment is central to our work. We make no pretense, nor do we advocate, that certain types or forms of adult relationships are any more adaptable than others. We explore the reality of relationships, whether between people of the same sex or opposite sex, with the goal of understanding those that endure. For the purposes of research, there are no good or bad relationships, functional or dysfunctional relationships, normal or pathological relationships—only relationships to be understood. Our focus is on the subjective experiences of partners to each other as they live out their lives together.

Our professional investment in studying lasting adult relationships, which are central to personal development and well-being, stems from each author's experience of being married for more than thirty-five years. Along with other differences, our sexual orientations differ from individuals who volunteered to participate in this research. Awareness of our own backgrounds and values, as well as discussion of them as a research team, enabled us to accept those differences as we worked toward the goal of understanding the human phenomena of lasting relationships.

We use a multidimensional perspective for exploring and understanding how these partners adapted to each other over time and how relationships developed over the years. In the first chapter we discuss the theoretical frame that guided the research. Studies of same-sex relationships are limited. Until recent years, relatively little attention has been paid to the study of gay and lesbian relationships and even less to relationships that have lasted more than five years. The perspective includes the nature of partner roles, relational fit, the quality of their communication including decision making, conflict and its management, sexual and psychological intimacy, and the importance of support from family, friends, religion, and psychotherapy. Each of these relational themes is discussed in Chapters 2 through 7. In the final chapter, we discuss similarities and variations in the lasting relationships of same-sex and heterosexual couples.

Throughout the book we have taken great care in protecting the privacy of the people who were exceedingly generous in sharing their lives with us and with you, the reader. Any information that would have violated confidentiality has been disguised or omitted from the book. In that spirit we have used pseudonyms. For the sake of clarity, the pseudonyms of partners within a couple begin with the same letter.

Acknowledgments

The dream of a book becomes reality because of the contributions of many people. We want to acknowledge the contributions of our friends, colleagues, students, and family members who helped our dream come true. As part of our research team at Boston College, Joyce Aronson, Ph.D., Elizabeth Reuman Hemond, Ph.D., and Julie O'Rourke, Ph.D., conducted the interviews on which this book is based. Marissa Mezzanotte, Marguerite Tierney, and Dorothy Artesani Cochrane provided us with invaluable help. We also wish to thank the administration of the university, especially the deans of our respective schools, for their support. John Harney of Book Consultants of Boston encouraged and offered guidance to us as this project unfolded. We are indebted to the staff of Greenwood Publishing Group for their help, especially Lynn Zelem, Production Editor, and Frances Kianka, Copy Editor. To Congressman Barney Frank we extend thanks for his interest in and support of our work. Colleagues and friends who were generous in reading drafts of the manuscript and offering us feedback included Lou Benson, Dorigen Keeney, Joe Miglorie, and Jack Ward. To members of our families—Anna and Claudia Mackey, Evelyn and Mary O'Brien, Winifred and Richard Rome— we owe a special debt of gratitude, not only for the love that only families can offer but for their astute commentaries on our work.

1

Introduction

Neither of us see ourselves as traveling a path alone.

The voices in this book come from the stories of gay and lesbian partners who talk about their struggles over the years in building a life together. The stories reach beyond the obvious realities of sexual orientation to speak to the joys, sorrows, hopes, and fears of human beings who were committed to making their relationships work. You may come to know them, as we did, by listening to what they say about relationships that lasted for more than fifteen years. To a considerable extent, their stories are our stories.

This research has continuity with our previous studies of lasting relationships among heterosexual couples (Mackey and O'Brien 1995). Compared to marriages, relatively little research has been done on the development of same-sex relationships that have lasted ten years or more (Dorn 1991; Johnson 1991). Since the mid-1980s, there have been appeals for studies that would allow same-sex partners to tell their relationship stories through in-depth interviews (Peplau 1982, 1991).

Based on a life-span perspective, an interview guide was designed to explore how partners adapted in their relationships over the years. Each interview consisted of questions that focused upon dimensions of these relationships over time from the unique perspective of each partner. We asked respondents to tell us how their relationships developed over the years. The first few years of relationships have been identified as critical in forming a partnership that included negotiating roles and responsibilities (McWhirter and Mattison 1984; Clunis and Green 1993; Slater 1995); therefore, we suggested the first five years as a time frame for respondents, which we called the "early years." Around five years, an important transition occurs as partners consolidate the relational work of the early years (McWhirter and Mattison 1984). That consolidation of partnerships may extend over a second five-year period, which we referred to as the "middle years." If couples remain together for the first ten years without rupture of their relationships, research suggested that they are unlikely to break up (Blumstein and Schwartz 1983). After ten years, the development of relationships appears to be characterized by deepening of commitment, consolidation of the gains of the first decade, and collaboration in joint endeavors, which we called the "recent years."

The concept of years within a life-span perspective was a tool for exploring relationships over time but did not lock respondents into a rigid structure for telling us about: roles, relational fit, values, decision making, conflict and its management, sexual and psychological intimacy, as well as the significance of social supports to partners. This multidimensional approach for exploring relational development was grounded in a structure that did not interfere with or distort what respondents felt had actually happened in their lives together over the years. In fact, several respondents qualified their observations by pointing out that some dimensions of relationships may have extended beyond the five- or ten-year time marker. Given our objective of understanding how relational patterns developed over time and how partners adapted to each other, we could afford to be flexible without sacrificing consistency.

Details about our approach to collecting, coding, and analyzing the data may be found in Appendix A. The interview guide may be found in Appendix B.

In this chapter we review research that shaped the exploration of the development of specific dimensions in these relationships. The story of one couple in our study, Kate and Kristin, has been integrated into the review to illustrate the themes that will be discussed in subsequent chapters. We hope that excerpts from their story will add a human touch to the discussion of theory.

ONE COUPLE'S STORY: KATE AND KRISTIN

The themes that emerged from the story of Kate and Kristin were representative of the seventy-two stories in this book. Taken collectively, these individual stories form a fabric of themes that addressed: roles, relational fit, values, communication, decision making, conflicts and their management, psychological and sexual intimacy, and the significance of social supports in these lasting relationships. Kate and Kristin had been together more than twenty-five years. Both were in their sixties and had successful careers. Kate began her story by talking about what attracted her to Kristin. Similar to most couples in this study, Kate and Kristin came from different backgrounds. Kate's family valued civility in their relations. Reserved and polite, her parents set a tone of discretion about expressing personal feelings. As a consequence, Kate experienced considerable restraint in being open with Kristin about her feelings, especially angry ones arising from the disappointments and frustrations in the relationship. At the same time, her family valued respect and tolerance for others. Kate had always taken pride in her restraint, composure, and politeness before she met Kristin, who came from a blue collar family that communicated in loud, expressive ways that were described as "radically different" from Kate's. Kristin saw herself as uninhibited and direct in expressing her thoughts and feelings in contrast to the constrained personality of her partner.

Kate described how she viewed herself and Kristin:

> I was never one to show a lot of emotion, anger, or particular things like that. That's the way my family was. We grew up like that . . . her family was a very emotional family. Early on, through maybe the first and second five years, Kristin could be very vocal about something, and I would tend just to listen; sit back and not get my two cents worth in. When she would become upset about something or particularly verbal about something in the beginning, I would just be more inclined to retreat. Sort of like in a state of shock. Somewhere along the way I began to change. I do a much better job now of letting her know how I feel about something than I used to. I can pretty much give as good as I can take now. I'm still more of a let's wait and see, and she's more of a let's get in there and do something about it.

In this passage, Kate spoke of how an aspect of her behavior was modified even though she remained cautious, a "wait-and-see" person, when it came to solving problems. Even when specific behavior(s) were modified, remnants of old patterns remained. An important element in that process was that modifications needed to take place in the behavior(s) of each partner if higher levels of adaptation were to be realized. That type of behavioral modification was found in most relationships in our study.

Kristin described her perceptions about the relationship and how their family backgrounds shaped their roles, as well as the importance of differences to the quality of their life together. As obvious as their differences were, Kristin identified how similar each of them was at the level of core values, which enabled them to maintain a connection to each other when differences, alone, may have driven them apart:

> I'm the opposite which Kate finds attractive. She's very, very, very different . . . ethnically, religiously, and socially. I tend to be hyper, very high energy. She's very laid back, quiet, and calm. That can sometimes be deceptive. There's a lot of depth; there's a lot of intensity to Kate; it just comes out in very different ways. I think I was attracted to the stark differences, that kind of quiet calm assurance. I knew what kind of a person she was, where she was coming from.

At one level, the interpersonal behaviors of Kate and Kristin were dramatically different. At another level, their inner values about the centrality of the relationship in their lives and their empathy for each other were very similar. The complementary fit between them based on behavioral differences was an interpersonal reality for most couples in this study. Opposites were attracted to each other. Differences enabled individual partners to experience a sense of personal wholeness through their relationships. Each one found in the other qualities that were missing in themselves, an experience that had a complementary function in relationships. For example, the "quiet calm" of Kate was experienced as "very reassuring and soothing" to Kristin, who had a volatile temperament.

Of significance in understanding the quality of and satisfaction with relationships was the way in which roles were negotiated between partners. The dynamics in negotiating roles were particularly important in view of the lack of same-sex role models for gay and lesbian relationships. As a consequence, gays and lesbians may rely on heterosexual relationships for working out their roles, which may not be appropriate for them (Carl 1990). On the one hand, a lack of models on which to organize same-sex relationships created stress in negotiating finances and in allocating household responsibilities (Driggs and Finn 1990). On the other hand, an absence of models offered partners a unique opportunity for negotiating roles that met their different needs. McWhirter and Mattison (1984) observed that partners were free to experiment with developing roles that met their individual and relational needs. On a similar theme, Blumstein and Schwartz (1983) suggested that same-sex couples, like heterosexual couples, had more options than previous generations for adopting relational roles not based on traditional expectations.

With the advent of research focused on the unique aspects of women's development, challenges have been made to traditional gender-linked roles. A social shift has been occurring toward flexible egalitarian roles for men and women in relationships (Faderman 1991). In our study, dual careers and joint incomes provided some degree of economic independence, relational equity, and a balance of power between partners. Economic independence, personal autonomy and a responsibility for one's own well-being, and an emphasis on equity and income separation have been important issues for lesbian couples (Blumstein and Schwartz 1983).

An important aspect of relationships was the complementary nature of role behaviors between partners. Kate and Kristin spoke of their relationship as a complementary one when they described their differences. For them, complementarity was based on their individual backgrounds, which shaped behavioral characteristics that each partner brought to the relationship. Studies have found similar relational patterns as those identified by Kate and Kristin in which complementary roles were shaped by the talents and skills of individual partners, which were important factors in relational stability and satisfaction (Kurdek 1993; McWhirter and Mattison 1984).

Kate and Kristin spoke of the dynamic nature of roles in their relationship. In addition to individual talents and skills, their roles were shaped by mutual adaptations to circumstances and changes in their careers. Kate described how she assumed additional responsibilities at home when Kristin needed to devote more energy and time to her career. She also identified the reciprocal exchange between them. If one partner was unavailable to carry out her responsibilities, the other would step in:

> What I tried to do was help her when she would get so involved, by doing some other things around here. By the same token, when

I got very involved in my work, we switched roles. She did the laundry. She did the things that from time to time I had done for her when she would get so involved.

Kate also described how changes in health required them to make adaptations in roles that had been decided in the past by the individual talents and skills of each partner:

We always laugh that I have become the "butch" because of her health. There are some things that she can't do and shouldn't do, and so I'm doing some of the lifting and the heavy stuff. We have always shared a lot in the day-to-day responsibilities. I may be doing more now than I was because of the things Kristin can't do.

Kristin described how their roles needed to be modified because of her health problems:

I've always valued that we both seem to be very easy with letting each do the things we like to do; our interests lie in some different areas. . . . I used to do a lot of woodworking and refinishing of furniture. That's been very hard for me to give up. . . . What I have tried to do is to find ways to keep my quality of life as much like it always has been, but without much risk taking. That has changed some of the roles because I would be the one to fix things. . . . Those are things that Kate either doesn't have any interest in or proclivities toward; at this point, we do have lots of workmen, but it still pisses me off that I have to pay somebody to do some minor things.

Delineating roles in the relationship was worked out between Kate and Kristin as their relationship evolved. Except for periods when career responsibilities compromised the time available at home, their individual talents, skills, and interests were the determining factors in allocating roles, a finding comparable with existing research on the subject (Blumstein and Schwartz 1983; Kurdek 1993; Maracek, Finn, and Cardell 1982; McWhirter and Mattison 1984; Tuller 1978). When Kristin's health began to deteriorate in recent years, they renegotiated who would be responsible for tasks that had been assumed by her over the years. Flexibility and commitment by each partner to the relationship were vital resources in adapting to these changes that were beyond their control. In previous research, personal preference, talent, skill, and time have been identified as more important to adaptation in lesbian relationships than adherence to particular roles (Blumstein and Schwartz 1983; Lynch and Reilly 1986).

Similarities in relational values—especially trust, respect, and equity—were also important to the viability of Kate and Kristin's relationship. Where complementary differences had the potential to drive partners apart, symmetry in these values, along with a commitment toward building mutual understanding and sensitivity, enabled them to preserve the relationship even during the most stormy periods. Although they maintained mutual respect for each other, Kristin commented on how trust was tested severely during the middle years of their relationship. As a consequence of great differences between them, Kristin felt increasingly estranged from Kate. Kristin talked about the effect of an affair during the middle years on the trust between them:

> High professional respect was there from the start in the sense that it was one of the things that drew us together. It went through a lot of tests and a lot of ups and downs in those first years. . . . She felt that her trust in me had been terribly violated when I got involved in an affair. I think we had to work really hard to restore that . . . because of a lot of personal early childhood history, family history, other stuff, baggage that you bring into a relationship, I really didn't trust her. I didn't trust anybody, and it was like I would knee jerk into a lot of old ancient patterns that had nothing to do with our relationship . . . talking things through became a mode of operating that's been really critical, but to say just talking would be simplistic. It was the trust that built up over the years, the bridges that we built in less intense areas; that finally let me trust.

Kate expressed how trust evolved over the years as they worked toward mutual understanding. For Kate and Kristin, their commitment to mutual reflection on their relational conflicts contributed to building a trustful openness. After Kristin's sexual affair, which occurred during the middle years of their relationship, it took several years before trust was restored. Although discussion was helpful in restoring trust, the processing of their experiences was "necessary but not sufficient" to repair the relational wound.

> I think we both trust each other. I don't know that I always did, but as time went on, I got to know Kristin better; we got to know each other better . . . it wasn't to the degree that it is now, but I think that's a very important part of it. I've never had any

indication that she didn't have complete trust in me. I think that
my trust in her has grown. Before when I was talking about trust,
I guess I was talking about . . . just the sexual trust. I mean trust
period, now!

Compared to gays, lesbians in this study spent more time and effort
in processing their relational experiences, which, for Kate and Kristin,
led to a deepening of mutual trust, respect, and empathy. Although
research on interpersonal processing of relational experiences by gay
and lesbian partners was not conclusive, women's developmental research has hypothesized that relational attachments are valued differently by women than by men. Continuity of meaningful attachments
rather than autonomy has been central to the developmental well-being
of women (Chodorow 1978; Gilligan 1982; Miller 1984; Surrey 1984,
1987). Interpersonal relationships nurtured by empathy and interde-
pendency have been essential to women's development. There has been
much discussion about fusion in lesbian relationships based on hypotheses that have emerged from women's developmental research.
Fusion as an element in lesbian relationships (Burch 1982; Krestan and
Bepko 1980) has been characterized by high levels of self-disclosure
between partners (Slater and Mencher 1991). Elise (1986) found that
lesbian partners tended to merge emotionally, while gay partners
maintained emotional distance from each other.

Some of the discrepancies in these findings may be related to how
attachment and autonomy were defined operationally, what they meant
to men and women within the context of committed same-sex relationships, and how they were measured. Our use of interviews in which
individual partners expressed the meaning of attachment and autonomy
in their own words within the context of their relationships produced
a rich understanding of these processes. While it was true that lesbians
in this study spent more time than gays in processing their relational
experiences, most lesbians were forthright in describing the importance
of autonomy within the attachments to their partners. For these
women, autonomy needed to be understood within the context of
meaningful attachments grounded on relational values, such as trust,
respect, and empathy. They valued their individual autonomy within
the contexts of committed relationships. Kristin reflected on the theme
of symmetry in relational values as she described the relationship with
Kate:

> Though we were very different, there was an incredible compatibility in terms of values. We may have some personality differences or some tempo differences, but in terms of the basic, fundamental things in life, I thought we were very compatible. . . .
> One of the things we've learned over the years is that if you look at us on the surface . . . it would look like we were much more polarized than we, in fact, are.

Shared values of commitment, trust, respect, empathic understanding, and equity enabled partners to negotiate differences and to contain conflict about differences at tolerable levels. Even more important, symmetry in values nurtured a sense of mutuality between partners who were different in many ways. Similar to values in heterosexual relationships, mutuality in trust, respect, and understanding have been instrumental to the development of satisfying same-sex relationships (Blumstein and Schwartz 1983; McWhirter and Mattison 1984; Rempel, Holmes, and Zanna 1985; Kurdek 1988a). Although equity has been associated with the quality of relationships in general, it has a special significance for lesbians. Kate commented on the significance of equity and fairness:

> It balances. With some things, probably, I let Kristin take an unfair share, so it's not fair in that particular situation . . . like our relationship with other people. I think overall it just balances out. Some areas, she is more there than I am. Other areas, I'm more there than she is. . . . We've been able to talk it through though . . . it's really difficult for things not to be fair.

A fair balance in what partners contributed to and took from relationships was a prominent theme as lesbian respondents discussed roles, household duties, finances, and decision making. Equity has been identified as a central value in all relationships that last, especially those of lesbians (Blumstein and Schwartz 1983; Lynch and Reilly 1986; Kurdek 1988a; Peplau 1982; Schneider 1986). Fairness in deciding about roles, household responsibilities, and finances has been linked to relational satisfaction. Valuing and achieving equity were not the same. Although research has found that most partners thought of equity as an important value, only a minority of partners reported that it characterized their relationships (Caldwell and Peplau 1984; Reilly and Lynch 1990).

The achievement of a sense of equity has been associated with mutuality in decision making among heterosexual and same-sex couples (Howard, Blumstein, and Schwartz 1986). When partners in a relationship have felt relatively equal in their capacity to influence decisions, decision making has been characterized by negotiation and discussion (DeCecco and Shively 1978). Such an equitable distribution of power was supported by relational values of mutual trust and respect, which, despite conflict based on interpersonal differences, characterized the decision making of Kate and Kristin. Kate spoke of how mutual respect contributed to equitable negotiations in making decisions:

> There are some things that I feel strongly about, but it's pretty easy for me to go along. I respect Kristin's point of view on some things, and I think she respects mine. We try to see each other's point of view when there is some kind of a difference. Sometimes we do it her way and sometimes we do it my way. . . . Neither of us see ourselves as traveling a path alone.

Kristin talked of a similar theme about their approach to making decisions but identified how personal differences had the potential to undermine mutuality in decision making:

> We were always very committed to making joint decisions from the start, both of us. . . . But Kate takes a long time to make decisions. I tend to be sort of thoughtful and strategic and she's sort of thoughtful and deliberate. . . . That was such a real sticking point. She would feel like: "Stop, you're breathing down my neck; leave me alone!" I would feel like: "How deliberative can you be?; you're in a paralysis!"

Effective communication has been recognized as a vital resource in making decisions, solving problems, and strengthening interpersonal bonds in all relationships. Differences in the patterns of communication have been linked to the relational orientations of men and women. Women have an orientation toward attachment and men toward autonomy in relationships; these different orientations lead to differences in their patterns and quality of communication (Tannen 1990). In same-sex relationships, however, studies have found no significant differences between gays and lesbians on measures of dyadic attachment and personal autonomy (Kurdek and Schmitt 1986; Peplau 1981). In fact, high dyadic attachment and low personal autonomy have been associated with the quality of relationships, a positive aspect of which was effective communication.

The research literature was not conclusive about the quality of communication in same-sex relationships. Some studies have found emotional distancing (Levine 1979) and impaired communication (George and Behrendt 1987) between gay partners; McWhirter and Mattison (1988) found that gays "over communicate" with each other during the early years of their relationships. After a decline in the quality of communication during the middle years, gay partners experienced a "renewal" of positive communication in their later years.

Although gays and lesbians, in our study, did not differ significantly in their decision-making styles, their patterns of communication over the years were quite different. Openness, honesty, and comfort in talking with one's partner characterized communication in half of all relationships during the early years. Positive communication remained at the same level between lesbian partners but dropped sharply between gay partners in the middle years. By recent years, about one out of two gays and four out of five lesbians viewed their communication as positive.

The differences between gays and lesbians in communication patterns appeared to have been connected to the orientation of lesbian partners to process mutually their relational experiences. Gay partners did not talk in the same way about the value and importance of mutually reflecting on what had occurred in their relationships. After acknowledging her difficulties with face-to-face discussion about relational matters, Kate described Kristin as "insisting" that they "sit down and talk about things." Kristin had "no question that we had to work on this relationship . . . we really had to talk about what I needed from her and what she needed from me." Not infrequently, as with this couple, one partner was a catalyst for ongoing dialogue about their relationships.

In all relationships that last, interpersonal conflict is inevitable as it was in these relationships. Heterosexual, gay, and lesbian couples have been found to differ on similar issues (Blumstein and Schwartz, 1983), which, without mutual resolution, may evolve into major conflict. Confronting issues that divided partners has been usually more effective in preventing the emergence of major conflict (Gottman 1991) than persistent avoidance, which has led to unresolved tensions and dissatisfaction (Levinger 1979; Baucom, Notarius, Burnett, and Haefner 1990).

In our study, the proportion of lesbians who described major conflict over the years was higher than for gays. During the middle years, for example, 58 percent of lesbians compared to 46 percent of gays reported major conflict, defined by us as interpersonal problems that were distressing to a respondent and that had a disruptive effect on the quality of relationships. Conflict often emerged as a result of personality differences, as was the case in Kate and Kristin's relationship. Among lesbian couples, differences in incomes and in the handling of finances frequently led to conflict. By the current phase, the numbers of all respondents who reported major conflict in their relationships had declined substantially.

An important aspect in understanding adaptation over time was the ways in which conflict was managed. We had the unusual opportunity to understand how partners in both same-sex and heterosexual relationships managed conflict (Mackey and O'Brien 1995). Studies have shown that women withdraw rather than remain in friendships with other women in which there are personal differences (Lever 1976; Eichenbach and Orbach 1988). However, studies of marriage have shown that wives are more likely than husbands to confront interpersonal differences (Burke, Weier, and Harrison, 1976; Huston and Ashmore 1986; Mackey and O'Brien 1995; Wills, Weiss, and Patterson 1974). Patterns of avoidance were evident in how Kate talked about her predominant style of managing conflict:

> When there was something that needed to be talked about, that was a little hot, I would tend to retreat. I would not do it . . . in the beginning I was more inclined to give in. As we've been together over time, I've become more assertive about getting my opinion and my feeling out, than I was at one time.

Balancing the avoidant style of Kate was the confrontative style of Kristin. These types of personality differences in managing conflict were not unusual and often led to higher levels of satisfaction in recent years. The role of the confrontative partner was to put the conflictual agenda on the table so that the issue that divided partners could be discussed and worked out. Of great importance to the process of modifying avoidant behaviors was mutual understanding and acceptance. As a consequence, modifications took place in the roles each partner played in relationships. Kristin commented on the process of modifying behaviors over the life of their relationship:

> We were always very civilized with each other, but our styles are vastly different. I am confrontational. . . . Most people would not believe how I hated being confrontational when I have to. But if I have to, then I can do it. That was her style, and I had my style . . . in the middle of the most horrific, mudslinging campaign, she was able to remain calm. That was hard . . . the rest is just hard work. We learned. We learn one thing and we keep learning it again and again. . . . You've got to take care of business. There is no easy way. When you forget, that is when you get in trouble.

For many couples, psychotherapy was an instrumental resource in developing effective communication, more so for lesbians than for gays. Four out of five lesbian couples and one out of four gay couples utilized professional help in working out their relational conflicts.

Because of the lack of studies of same-sex relationships that last more than five years, relatively little information was available in the literature to guide an exploration of intimacy over the life span of relationships. We defined psychological intimacy as the sharing of personal thoughts and feelings with one's partner that one would not ordinarily express to someone else. Psychological intimacy has been correlated with emotional expressiveness and trust (Kurdek 1988a) as well as with a mutual sense of equity about relationships (Eldridge and Gilbert 1990; Kurdek 1988a; Peplau 1982). We also explored the physical aspects of being intimate with one's partner, which included genital sex as well as physical embracing, touching, and hugging.

Because research suggested that gay partners had sex outside their relationships more than lesbian partners, we explored patterns of monogamy. Our finding resonated with those of other researchers that most gay partners had sex outside their relationships (Blumstein and Schwartz 1989; Harry 1984; Kurdek and Schmitt 1985/86; McWhirter and Mattison 1984). Some studies suggested that these gay partners have been together longer than those who maintain monogamous relationships (Blasband and Peplau 1985; Harry 1984; Kurdek and Schmitt 1985/86; McWhirter and Mattison 1984) and hypothesized that sexual openness may, therefore, facilitate stability in gay relationships. Gay partners have reported similar levels of relational satisfaction whether or not they have sex outside their relationships. Lesbians reported higher levels of satisfaction with their relationships when they were monogamous (Kurdek 1991a).

In our earlier research on lasting marriages (Mackey and O'Brien 1995), we found an inverse relationship between the quality of sexual

intimacy and psychological intimacy as heterosexual couples lived out
their lives together. A similar pattern from early to recent years was
found in these same-sex relationships. Kate spoke of that theme:

> In the beginning, sex was very important and quite frequent.
> Gradually it's diminished. That used to worry us, that we didn't
> find ourselves as frequently involved as we formerly had or as we
> thought we should. We would talk about it. Now, we think about
> something sexual as bigger than the sex act: the caring, the
> feeling, the understanding that we have for each other . . . it's too
> bad that people, when they talk about homosexuals or lesbians,
> they think about just the sex act, when it's really a way of life. It's
> a relationship. There's so much more to it really. That used to worry
> us, that we're not that active sexually, but I think it doesn't worry
> us as much now.

Kristin's perspective about intimacy had both similarities and differences from Kate's. She began by referring to the differences between
them about sexual relations:

> The biggest adjustment was that she was not as interested in sex
> as frequently as I was. That was hard. . . . I didn't like it. I resented
> it. Sometimes the sex was wonderful and sometimes it was not so
> wonderful. . . . One of the things that I have learned over the years,
> about my own personal relationship as well as just thinking about
> the whole area of sexuality, is that there's more than just genital
> sex. If you get stuck on just talking about genital sex, then if that
> doesn't stay up in terms of frequency and intensity, it's sort of like
> oh my God, where are we? . . . I couldn't even tell you how and
> when that changed. It didn't change with us having a lot more
> sex. It changed with us having a different perspective about it.

Compared to more than 75 percent of respondents who remembered their sexual relations as positive in the early years, less than half
responded similarly during recent years. Lesbians viewed their sexual
relations less favorably than gays throughout all three phases. More
lesbians than gays reported a sense of psychological intimacy over the
life span of their relationships. While psychological intimacy remained
constant among gays through the middle years, it declined among
lesbians. No doubt, that decline was a consequence of an increase in
major conflict between lesbian partners in the middle years. During
recent years, there was an appreciable difference between gays and

lesbians in the quality of psychological intimacy; more lesbians spoke positively about that dimension of their relationships. The differences in the patterns of sexual and psychological intimacy reflected gender differences about these two aspects of intimacy.

Social support from families and friends as well as from institutions, such as churches and synagogues, have been important resources for stability and quality in heterosexual marriages (Lewis and Spanier 1979). Because other researchers have found that same-sex couples have not received levels of social support comparable to heterosexual couples (Carl 1990; Driggs and Finn 1990), we explored how respondents perceived family, church, and friends as sources of support for their relationships. Studies have shown that gays and lesbians have experienced a cutoff in support from their families once they have "come out" and that support from friends was instrumental in their relational adjustments and the reduction of psychological distress (Blumstein and Schwartz 1983; Kurdek 1988b; Kurdek and Schmitt 1987b). In their study of gay relationships, however, McWhirter and Mattison (1984) did not report similar correlations between social support of family and friends and patterns in relational and personal well-being.

Friends became the most important source of social support to the couples in our study. Respondents often talked about friendships as if they were family, an observation that may have reflected that families were not accepting and affirming of these relationships. As Kate observed: "we've created some extended families that are not blood families . . . if the chips are down, we're all right there . . . that's been very special for us." Although more families of gays were supportive than those of lesbians in the early years, less than half of all families were seen as supportive even during recent years. Churches and synagogues, like families, were not perceived as supportive resources by the majority of respondents, despite some notable exceptions. As respondents grew older, many talked of an interest in their spiritual lives that usually transcended denominational lines.

An important source of social support, which we have already pointed out, was the widespread use of couples psychotherapy, especially among lesbian couples. Therapy was clearly linked to the well-being of partners and the quality of their relationships.

DEVELOPMENT OF RELATIONSHIPS OVER TIME

Few studies have investigated the development of lasting relationships among lesbian and gay couples who remained committed to their relationships for more than a few years (Kurdek and Schmitt 1986; Kurdek 1992). Studies frequently relied on survey techniques in contrast to the focal question interviews we employed.

One study that used interviews to explore relational development was conducted with gay couples in the 1970s (McWhirter and Mattison 1984). Based on interviews with 156 gay couples who had been together for one to thirty-seven years, McWhirter and Mattison proposed a six-stage model for understanding how relationships evolved over time. The first year was a "blending" period in which partners formed a relationship based on perceived similarities. A sense of mutual tranquillity characterized most, if not all, aspects of their relationships. After this period of blending, mutuality declined as the realities of negotiating differences and coping with household tasks were faced. This period, which was referred to as "nesting," lasted into the third year when a new developmental agenda of "maintaining" the relationship became a focal issue. During the third stage, balances needed to be worked out between the needs of individual partners and those in their relationships; differences often resulted in more conflict during this third stage than in earlier stages. If couples were able to navigate their way through the first five years of their relationships, they entered a five-to-ten-year "collaborating" period characterized by a "settling in" theme in which the need to negotiate relational differences and conflict was no longer a primary focus. The last two stages, which occurred after couples had been together more than ten years, reflected a maturing of relationships. From ten to twenty years, "trust" developed and was often manifested in joint ownership of possessions; during this second ten years, a danger was in taking relationships for granted. The beginning of a sixth stage, "repartnering," marked the twentieth anniversary of a couple, when there was a renewal of commitment to the relationship.

The work of McWhirter and Mattison was helpful in organizing our approach to exploring the development of lesbian and gay relationships that had lasted more than fifteen years. However, their research focused only on gays and was conducted in an era considerably different from the 1990s. As a consequence, we did not rely only on their results, particularly their finding of specific time-limited stages for under-

standing the development of relationships. Their work helped in for-
mulating questions about our data: Would early years in our study be
characterized by the harmony and minimal conflict that McWhirter and
Mattison had found? Would the second five years be as conflict-free and
collaborative between partners as it had been in their study? Would the
recent years be characterized by consolidation of trust and commitment
to relationships?

There have been no systematic studies of relational development
among lesbian couples who have been together for more than fifteen
years, although recent studies suggested that "45% to 80%" of lesbians
were in ongoing relationships (Peplau 1991). Researchers have focused
on relationships lasting less than ten years and have relied on mail
questionnaires to compare aggregate data about partners (Kurdek and
Schmitt 1986; Kurdek 1988a, 1992).

Slater and Mencher (1991) identified several challenges and stresses
that were unique in the lives of lesbian couples. While acknowledging
that lesbian and heterosexual couples followed similar stages in relational development, the authors emphasized the importance of attend-
ing to critical differences between the two groups because lesbian
relationships lack cultural supports in the form of rituals and markers
that offer social validation and support to heterosexual relationships.
The observations of Slater and Mencher were not only helpful in
identifying recurrent stresses in lesbian relationships, but in understanding the difficulties of using rigid time frames to understand the
development of relationships.

Unlike the McWhirter and Mattison formulation of stages, recent
work on the development of lesbian relationships has hypothesized
identifiable stages without specific time frames. This theoretical work
on a developmental model for understanding lasting relationships of
lesbian couples relied on anecdotal evidence from therapeutic relationships and friendships and on the observations of colleagues (Clunis and
Green 1993; Slater 1995). Clunis and Green (1993), like McWhirter
and Mattison, proposed that lesbian relationships evolved through six
stages: in the first stage, "prerelationship," individual partners con-
tended with the task of how involved each wished to be in the new
relationship, including whether or not to sexualize it. If the choice was
to become involved with each other, the relationship entered a second
stage, "romance," which was characterized by a sense of oneness and
fusion between the partners. As the glow of romantic connectedness
dimmed with the recognition of differences, a third stage of "conflict"

ensued. The threat of that conflictual stage was disillusionment, which could result in the termination of the relationship unless differences between the partners were resolved. If conflicts were negotiated in a mutually satisfactory way for each partner, a stage of "acceptance" emerged in which there was an integration of couple connectedness and individual separateness within the relationship. The integration of these two opposing forces led to greater "commitment" to the relationship, which was the fifth stage in the Clunis and Green model. With the relationship grounded in a renewed sense of commitment, partners entered a sixth stage in which they collaborated on tasks that contributed to the well-being of others. This process model hypothesized that individual, couple, and social factors led to variability in the length of stages and how stages sequenced over the life of relationships.

Another model for understanding the development of lesbian relationships was proposed by Slater (1995). It was based on data similar to those in the Clunis and Green model, that is, from psychotherapy clients, friends, and families. Slater argued that a single model for understanding all relationships was unrealistic in view of the personal, relational, social, and cultural diversity among lesbian couples. She did not specify time frames for each of the five stages in her model of intact lesbian relationships. In stage one, "the formation of the couple," the bliss of being in love obscured potential conflict between the partners. Because each partner was invested in building a meaningful relationship yet fearful of losing it, the couple avoided conflict that was perceived as a threat to the relationship. With the development of a trustful attachment between partners, the couple began to experiment with modes of negotiating differences. As partners became aware of personal differences between them, the initial glow of the first stage faded. Confronting personal differences was a threat to the viability of their life together, but it also offered them an opportunity to deepen their relationship, which led to a decision to live together and to a vow of monogamy. A primary task of the second stage, which was referred to as "ongoing couplehood," was to develop modes for managing individual needs for togetherness and separateness, closeness and distance. The third stage, or "the middle years," which included both the chronological ages of partners as well as the state of their relationship, was characterized by a consolidation of commitment to the relationship. Although commitment reinforced relational stability, there was a threat of relational stagnation as partners became accepting of individual differences. The challenge was to find ways of bringing excitement to the relationship. An outcome of that challenge was to contribute to a wider cause, the fourth stage, which Slater referred to as "generativity," in which partners became involved in lesbian and gay groups oriented to social action. The fifth stage, "lesbian couples over 65," included retirement from employment. The loss of employment by one or both partners required a renegotiation of their relationship. Almost inevitably, themes of togetherness and separateness and the impending reality of death, no matter how far away, played an important role in renegotiating relationships.

These three models of relational development provided benchmarks for our research. We considered the formulations about stages to be hypotheses that were a foundation upon which to design our approach for exploring and understanding lasting same-sex relationships. McWhirter and Mattison (1984) hypothesized stages within specific time periods in contrast to other theorists (Clunis and Green 1993; Slater 1995), who identified tasks within stages not framed by specific time periods. Based on these works, we decided to explore relational processes within time frames that served as flexible markers over the life span of these relationships.

SUMMARY

Existing research was used to identify the kinds of questions that were asked in these interviews. Based on the observations of other researchers, clinicians, and theorists, we adopted a life-span perspective for exploring the development of relationships between gay and lesbian partners. Roles, relational fit, values, conflict and its management, decision making, intimacy including psychological closeness as well as sexual relations, and the significance of social supports to relationships were explored. Findings from previous studies enabled us to structure the life span of these relationships into three periods: the early years covering approximately the first five years, the middle years that roughly included the next five years, and the recent years from ten years to the present time.

2

Roles

Friends would say, who's the husband, who's the wife? It was, like, neither of us.

The concept of social role was a useful tool in exploring how relationships evolved from the early years to the present time. We thought of roles as the patterns of behaviors between partners that connected them interpersonally in a relationship. The dynamics that fueled the adoption of various roles were complex. Past experiences with models were an important element of how one learned to behave in a relationship. Reciprocal patterns of behaviors within the context of the relationships themselves also contributed to the behavioral configuration of roles.

The quality of past experiences with primary figures in the lives of gays and lesbians had an influential effect in shaping their roles with partners. The selective qualities of role models with which individuals identified and which they then internalized had a powerful effect on interpersonal behaviors in these relationships. The qualities that partners carried with them into these relationships came primarily from experiences with parents. Other figures who were mentioned less frequently included other heterosexual couples, gay and lesbian couples, historical figures, and literary characters.

A second element in shaping roles—the interactions of partners over time—was a reciprocal process: individuals were simultaneously affecting the behavior of a partner and being affected by a partner without necessarily being aware of what was transpiring between them. These interrelated patterns of behaviors had a shaping effect on the development of roles. This chapter explores how relationships were shaped by role models and partner interactions over time.

ROLE MODELS

All of us—children, youth, and adults—look to others for cues in finding our way through current relationships. We incorporate into our emerging sense of self those qualities of important figures that help us structure our roles with others. Theory suggests that primary figures of identification, who are most influential as role models, are in our families of origin. Our research explored who gays and lesbians looked to as figures of identification for structuring their roles with their partners. All respondents had grown up in families in which the orientation of parents toward sexuality was of a heterosexual nature. The heterosexual orientation of a parent was not important to the process of identification and internalization. Rather, gays and lesbians talked about specific qualities within mothers and fathers with which they identified regardless of the sex or the sexual orientation of the parent.

Seventy-seven percent of lesbians and 62 percent of gays reported that they were similar, in at least some ways, to one or both parents. Rarely did individuals see themselves as totally similar to a parent. Admirable qualities that one wished to emulate were selected, while others were rejected. Fifty-six percent of lesbians described their similarities to parents in mixed terms: they identified with selective qualities in a parent and rejected other qualities, or they identified with what they perceived as admirable qualities in one parent while rejecting the negative qualities of the other parent. Gays were more likely to reject parents as role models: 38 percent of gays compared to 23 percent of lesbians said that there were no similarities between them and a parent.

Betsy, who has been with her partner for twenty-eight years, talked about memories of important experiences with her mother:

> When I was a kid, my mother shared with me a couple of attitudes that she had gotten from her father that had to do with sexuality between creatures. . . . I happened to have a spayed female dog

that liked to mount other females. So I was given a very serious explanation that this is the way of nature and this sometimes happens and it's OK. So I didn't have a particular problem. . . . I didn't feel any revulsion or anything, or being a real oddity. So when I recognized this within myself, it was just a natural thing. No big deal. I didn't know at the time that this was supposed to be bad.

A quality in Betsy's mother as a model was related to attitudes toward homosexuality. The specific incident of the female dog mounting another female dog seemed to crystallize in Betsy's mind the naturalness and acceptability of same-sex behavior that was passed on to her through the accepting attitudes of her mother. Attitudes about sexuality, modeled by her mother, allowed Betsy to feel accepting of herself as a lesbian. Betsy comments further on the significance of her mother as a role model:

When dad had to be on special diets, she used to try and invent special things he could have that would be on his diet so that he wouldn't have to feel like he was a sick person . . . they really were interested in each other and they wanted to do things to make the other person happy. . . . I'm just as stoic sometimes as my mother. I know my mother taught me how to take care of a sick person. She was an excellent nurse, amateur nurse.

Betsy identified with her mother as a stoic yet nurturing person, especially as she took care of her husband. She admired and respected how her parents did things for each other and how they tried to please each other. Qualities of caring for a loved one, which she had observed in her mother, became part of her role with Beverly.

Beverly also identified with qualities in her parent's relationship that were later integrated into the relationship with Betsy. The sensitivity, caring, and spirit of compromise that she observed in her parent's relationship became part of her life with Betsy. Beverly spoke of these themes in the following excerpt:

My parents have a very similar relationship to ours. My mother and father have been married for fifty-five years and they're each other's best friends. It's the same sort of thing. My mother used to talk with me about compromise and how my dad would compromise a lot with her, but there were certain things that he just wouldn't; if that was that, then she said: "OK that's it. There's so few things that he won't compromise . . . we both like each other. We're each other's best friends." When my mother said that, I laughed because we say that all the time to each other. There's a lot of respect and a lot of trust. A lot of caring about the other one. Not putting the other's needs above yours but certainly putting them right up there equal . . . and maybe sometimes above . . . there's a willingness to compromise when that's necessary.

Admired qualities that were perceived in a parent became valued resources as partners worked out relationships. At the same time, other qualities were rejected. Individuals who had negative memories of their parents' relationships did not want to repeat similar patterns in their relationships with their partners. A gay couple, who had been together for twenty years, described what they learned about relationships from experiences with their parents. In neither family were the parents remembered as positive figures. Barry's father was described as an alcoholic who was more interested in a career than in the family. In contrast, Barry retained a memory of his mother as an admirable figure who raised a large family by herself. Constantly reminded of the unhappiness in his parent's marriage, Barry struggled not to replicate the same qualities in his relationship with Brian:

My father was very weak . . . he wanted a career and not a family. My mother wanted a family and not a career. . . . She was very strong. She was on her own. Raised six children by herself . . . as a child growing up, I thought, if I ever got into a relationship, this would be what I wouldn't want in my life . . . my whole life was based on what I wouldn't want in a relationship. . . . My father was never loving to my mother. I am very loving to Brian. He's very loving to me and not afraid to show it at any time or any place . . . we both don't drink because we knew our parents were alcoholics. We just have sort of a fear about drinking. We probably could and it wouldn't bother us, but we don't. I think we're more open than they were.

Similar themes in the memories of his partner, Brian, were apparent as he talked about the relationship of his parents. Themes of emotional impoverishment and gross inequities in their marriage were apparent as Brian spoke of his determination not to repeat those qualities in his relationship with Barry:

Neither one of us comes from a family that provided a model. I know Barry's mother and father were not too happy and my mother and father were not too happy either. So I just think maybe the model we used was sort of an anti-model . . . maybe it did not work with them and we knew that being a couple took work, good love, and respect. It took a close commitment . . . we have seen a not so fine relationship in close range and . . . ours was not going to be like that. . . . I think my father came from the age of the domineering male and my mother came from the age of submissive females . . . there was an inequality there. I think that is deadly to a relationship. I think there has to be an equality. I really feel that Barry and I have that and they did not. . . . There are no similarities between our parents' relationships and our relationship. . . . None whatsoever. . . . Our relationship has so much respect and so much love and so much concern and so much caring.

In building a life together, this gay couple was trying to transcend the memories of unhappy experiences in their families so as not to repeat them in their relationship. Their observations illustrated how individuals compensated for the absence of positive role models in their lives. The challenge of not repeating negative relational patterns as perceived in the marriages of parents was complicated, because individuals had different experiences in their families. The key in adapting to those differences and in not allowing them to intrude into their relationships was through open and honest communication about what each partner wanted.

We also asked about other figures of identification who may have been important. Couples other than parents were mentioned, as were previous experiences in relationships. Keith talked about his search for role models:

When we first got together, we met two guys who are still together . . . they'd been together fifteen or seventeen years when we met them . . . we used them as a model. . . . These two guys had such a good time together, and they laughed a lot . . . they had this circle of straight and gay friends . . . they had such a happy life . . . an equal life . . . they seemed to give and take. . . . When we moved here, we met two other guys . . . they're very frugal, and they're both that way. But they're also very committed socially; they take on causes and they're very involved in the gay community. We use them as a model . . . just the commitment to each other, the commitment to society, the desire to leave the world a better place, the way they get so indignant when they are appalled by something. The way they're committed to each other is on the positive side, but the way they sort of keep this tally sheet makes us nuts. It's like we couldn't do that . . . we are more similar to a well-adjusted straight couple.

The relationship and lifestyle of the gay couple whom they met first were admired by Keith. Using them as models for building a relationship was timely, as he and his partner had recently met. Keith identified qualities in these role models that he admired while rejecting other qualities that were not so admirable. He and his partner identified with the commitment of the second gay couple as well as with their social activism, but at the same time they rejected the compulsive way in which the couple kept track of equity in their relationship. This process of selectively identifying with some qualities while rejecting other qualities in role models was common among respondents in this study.

Gay and lesbian role models were scarce during the years when people in this study were growing from adolescence into adulthood. Ken talked about the disadvantages along with the advantages of that reality:

In my late teens and early twenties I was a gay man, with sort of no reference points. I didn't know what a long-term relationship with another man was going to be all about. . . . Fifteen years later, I'm in a relationship that I see is as fulfilling, supportive, and loving as the relationship of my parents . . . there were some times when it would have been nice to have some role models to look to . . . but it was exciting to not have those role models and feel like there was nobody's societal constraints that we needed to fit into because we were, in the society at large, pariahs to begin with, so we really could make it up for ourselves . . . just because this worked for one couple doesn't mean that's what has to work for us. . . . We met a couple who had probably been together ten or twelve years . . . whom we became friendly with. . . . They were probably the most significant gay role model couple at that point . . . meeting and seeing them was significant as far as looking at a gay male couple who had been together for a significant period of time and who seemed to have some of the same values that we did. They went at life in similar ways, and they seemed to have some of the same agreements between the two of them that we did; the way they worked together, the way

> they divided responsibilities in their home, and just that they shared work together. We both also have our parents who have very loving, mutually supportive relationships . . . that's something I always looked toward. My parents love and respect each other and they had open lines of communication . . . so our relationship in some way, shape, or form looked like theirs.

In addition to their parents, Keith and Ken identified with a gay couple who had been together more than ten years. Each partner identified with values that resonated with their dreams for a happy life together. They also referred to the reality of no social expectations or constraints on gay relationships. The lack of expectations about relational roles offered them the opportunity to work out their relationship in ways that would be mutually satisfying to each partner. Rather than a liability, the freedom to develop a relationship without basing it on other relationships or societal norms was seen as an opportunity. In particular, this individual referred to the flexibility in partner roles that he felt was possible because there were few standards to which they needed to conform. This couple drew qualities, such as love, respect, and commitment, from several sources, to which they aspired in their relationship. In looking to other gay couples, they were reassured that a lasting and happy relationship could become a reality for them.

Some respondents found models of identification among heterosexual couples other than their parents. Abby, who has been in a relationship with Alicia for twenty years found a role model in friends:

> We have friends. . . . They have been together twenty-three or twenty-four years at this point. . . . In some ways they are a role model; they deal with hard things and they are good at communicating with each other. . . . Another couple that was a big influence on me when I was growing up was my choir director and his wife . . . they were people that I really looked up to and respected. I knew them from the time I was in third grade through high school. They seemed to be able to work together as well as to live together.

The selective nature of focusing on qualities in the relationships of others was apparent in what Abby said. Those qualities transcended gender and sexual orientation. Individuals admired the resiliency of others in not giving up when life got tough as well as the commitment of these couples to their relationships.

One out of four respondents had been married previously and used those relationships as benchmarks on which to build a life with their partners. Dana talked about the significance of her previous marriage and the hopes she had for the relationship with her partner:

> The only thing I wanted to do was have a better life than I had before. I think she did too. Her marriage didn't work and my marriage didn't work. You kind of feel like a failure no matter whose fault it was. But you want to make your life better than it was. So the only model that I had was to make it better than it was, to make a better life together. It isn't a rational thought, its just something that you do.

Most individuals who had been married talked similarly to Dana, who has been with Diane for twenty-five years. Despite strong feelings of failure that often mingled with conflicted feelings about adopting homosexual lifestyles and, as a consequence, accepting themselves as gay or lesbian, they persisted in building relationships with their partners. Their persistence in that journey was reinforced by a sense of hope that life would get better. Some individuals commented on features in their new relationships similar to those in previous relationships. Edward, who had been married twice, described the continuity in relational patterns between his marriages and the relationship with his partner, Evan, that has lasted twenty-two years.

> Surprisingly, both of my wives were the same. It is true you do marry the same people . . . yet . . . they're all totally different people. My first wife was a professional and did a lot of creative work . . . my second wife was very beautiful . . . she was very social; she too was passive/aggressive. Then I encountered Evan and I change my sexual orientation and wind up with somebody totally the same. . . . Our relationship has been very similar to a heterosexual relationship . . . when I look back at my first marriage we fell into the same kind of patterns as Evan and I have fallen into. . . . We've developed the same patterns as in my marriages . . . my wives were more social than I was . . . Evan is the same way. . . . So that's carried over to this. . . . My first wife was having a hard time; she became an alcoholic. . . . I had a hard time relating to that, forgiving her and helping her with it . . . that's what destroyed that relationship . . . the only common thing that might be would be Evan's extramarital affairs . . . by ignoring them is probably the way we've resolved it.

Edward commented on the similarities in the interpersonal patterns of dealing with conflict in these three relationships. Much of those patterns appeared to revolve around the avoidance of Edward in dealing directly with troublesome behavior in his wives and in his partner. Although the sexual affairs of Evan troubled Edward, he tried to ignore them, not unlike the way in which he had dealt with his first wife's alcoholism. The pattern of avoidance probably inflamed his anger and resentment as well as shame at having these feelings. Consequently, it became increasingly difficult to discuss these matters face to face. Unless modified, such a pattern in dealing with conflict may lead to estrangement in the connection between partners.

Evan also had been involved in previous heterosexual relationships. Similar to Edward, he felt that the sexual orientation of individuals had little or nothing to do with the quality of relationships. Referring to their relationship, Evan observed that, "the difference is that we're not public . . . it's pretty ordinary . . . intellectually, I know it's not ordinary, it's out of the ordinary." The discrepancy between how he experienced the relationship in reality and how he thought of it in the context of the predominant heterosexual culture was apparent. At one level, living with someone on a daily basis over an extended period of years was similar, regardless of the sexual orientations of the partners. At another level, when one put that relationship into the context of a world in which heterosexual values were dominant, one was confronted with significant differences. That theme was an ever-present reality in the lives of couples in this study.

A few respondents referred to figures in history and literature who were used as role models. References were made to admired people whom respondents aspired to emulate. After referring to the significance of her parents, whom she did not consider as positive models, Alice talked on that theme:

> I look to some of the bad things in my parents and say, that's exactly what I don't want to do in mine. . . . It's a model not to follow. I look at idealized models, like movies, and books, and stories about women in history. I look to Gertrude Stein and Alice B. Toklas as how not to be lesbian. Talk about roles. Gertrude Stein wrote the biography of Alice B. Toklas, and she totally dominated her. I wouldn't want to be like that. . . . We see romantic movies a lot. Neither of us can stand violent movies, so we see comedies or romances. We see things about relationships we can totally translate from heterosexual to gay. We don't need subtitles.

> We don't have to only see two women together to see love in
> relationships . . . one good thing about being gay, because if
> your parents are man and woman, and you're two women or two
> men, it just can't possibly be the same. You have to break out in
> order to come out. Intrinsic in being gay is the possibility, although
> certainly people can mimic and recreate the same fuck-ups that
> are in heterosexual parental marriages that they hate, but I think
> it leads you to be willing to question. I think that we really have
> questioned a lot of things. Our role models have been in books
> and movies.

In reflecting on her parent's marriage, Alice found few qualities that
she wished to incorporate in the relationship with her partner, Angela,
with whom she has been for twenty-three years. In fact, she viewed
them as "a model not to follow." She looked to others for cues on how
to go about developing a lesbian relationship. Although her models
were primarily from the relationships of lesbian couples, Alice also
commented on learning from observations of lovers in heterosexual
relationships. She referred to relational patterns and the underlying
themes between heterosexual partners with which she and other respondents resonated and wished to include in their own relationships.
Of even more importance were qualities of strength, caring, and
compassion among lesbian figures in the arts. An important part of the
process of using models to develop a relationship was the discussion
between partners that helped to clarify individual expectations; the
values of these figures helped to nurture the development of a sense of
mutuality between partners.

A few respondents reported that there were no figures in their
families, among other straight, gay, and lesbian relationships, or in
literature with whom they identified as models. Octavia and Olivia,
whose relationship has lasted eighteen years, spoke about the absence
of models in their lives. Octavia believed that:

> We really liked working from scratch and putting something
> together and kind of molded it. I really feel like we created it. I
> think we had ideal concepts like trust and respect but in terms of
> a model, no.

Many individuals referred to the reality of not knowing gay and
lesbian partners who had been in lasting relationships at the time when
they were starting their relationship. Olivia commented on that reality:

> We didn't know any lesbians who had been in a long-term relation-
> ship that we were sort of modeling ourselves after. I don't think it
> would be our parents, except for maybe the longevity issues and
> the commitment. But the relationship itself, I don't think so.

When most of these people met and started to develop relationships, gay and lesbian couples who could serve as role models were not readily available. It was not unusual, therefore, to find Olivia and others saying that they had not known of other gay and lesbian couples with whom they could identify. Although parents were the most commonly re-ported figures of identification, the voices of these lesbians and gays suggested many other sources on which they modeled their relation-ships.

RELATIONAL ROLES

In addition to the qualities perceived in relationships of others with whom one identified and wished to emulate, roles developed through communication with partners over time. The needs, talents, and expec-tations of a partner interacting with those of the other partner were highly influential in establishing patterns of behavior between them. This was a reciprocal process in which each partner was simultaneously affecting and being affected by the behaviors of the other partner.

One approach for understanding the structure of roles in these relationships was to view patterns of behavior along a continuum. At one end were instrumental behaviors and at the other, expressive behaviors. Patterns of behavior that we defined as instrumental were oriented to the accomplishment of tasks such as budgeting, cooking, and action(s) to reach a goal; individuals who were predominantly instrumental in their role behaviors were oriented to doing things. Expressive roles were oriented to sustaining relationships and included nurturing, listening, and supportive behaviors. We asked individuals about the behaviors they perceived in themselves and in their partners in order to understand the instrumental to expressive patterns of roles within their relationships. It is important for the reader to keep in mind that we are talking about the predominant patterns of behaviors that generally characterized the roles of individual partners in relationships.

Instrumental roles were stable throughout these relationships. The percentages of gay and lesbian partners who described themselves primarily as task-centered doers remained constant from the early years through recent years. Variations between gays and lesbians were apparent, however. Compared to the 31 percent of lesbians who were predominantly instrumental, 46 percent of gays described themselves that way from the early years of relationships to the recent years.

Compared to gays, more lesbians used language that described expressive behaviors when they talked about their roles. From the early years to the present, there was a slight increase in the percentage of lesbians who described their behaviors as predominantly expressive. In addition to instrumental and expressive roles, approximately 25 percent of each group used language that conveyed a mixture of instrumental and expressive behaviors throughout their relationships.

Although the roles of men and women were oriented differently for a sizable number of respondents in this study, the differences were not large. The variance between lesbians and gays was probably related to gender differences as, historically, men have tended to adopt instrumental roles and women expressive roles in relationships.

To clarify and deepen this overview of the structure of social roles, we looked beyond instrumental and expressive behaviors to explore how these partners tried to adapt to life together in a lasting relationship. Because there were no socially recognized norms on which they could base their relational behaviors as there were in heterosexual marriages, these partners were confronted with challenging relational agenda.

Gwen and Grace, who have been together nineteen years, talked about working out their roles. Gwen said:

> Neither one of us expect to fulfill any role. . . . We are not going to put roles on us. Women had always had to do that. By our natures we don't want that. I've always wished that Grace would cook more because I love to eat and I'm not a particularly good cook. I think it is the only thing I wish she'd like to do more. All the other junky stuff around the house I can do myself or she can do. We kind of naturally take up our certain things . . . we never expect that you have to do this or you have to do that.

Grace referred specifically to their rejection of role stereotypes, especially those of "butch/femme." We found little evidence of that stereotype having a significant and lasting effect on the structure of roles. Their personality differences resulted in considerable conflict between them. Grace spoke about the process of working out relational differences over the years:

> I remember we were very much against labels. On her part she
> would say she is opposed to this, but if she was going to be a
> role, she was absolutely the butch. If there was absolutely a role,
> I should be the femme. That fits my personality. . . . I have a whole
> different idea about it now, but then I thought about it as being
> the femme and attending to the details emotionally. We used to
> have big fights about it all through the 1970s. . . . I remember it
> being humorous about roles. It came up about cleaning. She and
> I have very different styles about how we organized tasks. She
> would get up early Saturday morning and clean and do all that
> kind of thing you were supposed to do before she would have
> fun. It would seem to me that if you were going to get up on
> Saturday and clean, why bother getting up. I would be much more
> interested in having a good time and then work the cleaning
> around the other things. . . . We always fight about cleaning. We
> finally hired somebody to clean to solve that problem.

Grace recalled the conflicts inherent in negotiating roles for which
there were few, if any, norms to guide them. During the 1970s when
they came together, butch/femme stereotypes were associated with the
structuring of roles in lesbian relationships. Their rejection of imposed
expectations about roles, coupled with the differences in personality
styles, provoked serious conflict between them. While differences did
not disappear, they were able to negotiate an accommodation to each
other. Openness to communicating about differences along with commitment to the relationship resulted in a deeper level of mutual
acceptance and respect. Gwen and Grace illustrated the process of
negotiation and accommodation many couples went through in working out roles.

Roles became organized most frequently as a consequence of the
talents and skills of partners. Florence and Felicia spoke of how their
different talents and skills had a significant effect on the roles each
partner adopted over the nineteen years of their relationship. Felicia
comments about the differing strengths each of them possessed, their
pragmatism in trying out new ways of being together, and their mutual
determination to avoid false expectations that did not fit with what they
wanted from the relationship:

> I guess that's the other thing in our relationship, it feels very equal
> even though we each have our own areas of expertise. . . . I don't
> think either one of us have expectations of behavior or how things
> should be set up so that the other gets measured against. We kind

of take things as they come and what works, rather than this is
how it should be or this is how we're going to make it be. I think
some of our friends have fallen into that trap.

Felicia spoke of specific ways in which talents and skills determined the
allocation of roles and responsibilities in their relationship:

I just thought I'd do the things that I did best. I like to cook, so I
thought well I'll cook. Florence is a terrible cook. I don't want her
to cook and that was a non-issue. Like, well of course you'll cook.
Florence didn't care about cooking. We sat down and said: "Who
will be the painter of ceilings in the house and negotiate it? Or
who does it better or who should do it?" There just wasn't a lot of
planning about that or there wasn't a lot of expectations that one
person versus the other person should do it. It was kind of like
who wanted to do it or who felt they were better at it.

Similar to Gwen and Grace, Florence and Felicia rejected stereotypical expectations for determining roles. They negotiated roles based on
the talents and skills of each partner. For lesbians, more than for gays,
negotiation was the route toward developing an agreement about who
would be responsible for specific tasks in the relationship. That process
could be conflictual as with Gwen and Grace, or it could unfold in a
fairly calm way as with Florence and Felicia. Personality traits had a lot
to do with how conflictual the process was.

Traits were an important dynamic in working out roles and responsibilities between partners. Based on one's intellectual and emotional
makeup, traits were dynamic characteristics that sometimes changed as
relationships developed. Jennifer and Joyce, who have been together
twenty-five years, spoke about personal traits that offered a beginning
structure to their relationship and how their roles changed as traits were
modified. Frequently, traits in each partner complemented those of the
other partner, as in the relationship of Jennifer and Joyce. Jennifer
pictured herself in the following way at the beginning of their relationship:

I was the caretaker. I think at the beginning of our relationship,
Joyce was the kind of emotional, insight person and I was kind
of like the learner. I was the physical caretaker person. Really was
kind of bad news when it started out like that. I think if we hadn't
gotten that adjustment we would have never lasted.

Jennifer, who came from a background as an instrumental caretaker of others, entered a new type of relationship with Joyce. Jennifer recognized early in the relationship that the imbalance in traits of each partner served both of their needs yet had the potential to harm, if not destroy, the relationship. As she began to develop her latent strengths, which had been dormant in previous relationships, both partners were confronted with the need to modify their roles. Joyce discussed how they renegotiated a different level of relatedness:

> When we started out I was a mentor and she was the mentee, so to speak, by the very nature of the age and life experience. . . . That worked for a while, and then she began to grow. She didn't want it that way anymore, and then I had to face the issue of letting go . . . that wasn't easy. . . . We really had to change things around as we started evolving. We didn't realize it at the time, but it was a very painful process. But I had to learn to let her be, and I had to learn how to be without having someone to take care of. I had to learn how to give to myself in a different kind of a way. She was learning how to be herself on her own. She no longer was feeling that need for a mentor. We became much more equal.

Initially, Jennifer, who was fifteen years younger than Joyce, assumed the role of a learner in the relationship. Joyce had more life experiences; as a consequence, she took on the role of mentor. As Jennifer's strengths emerged, which were fueled by successes in her career as well as by developments in their relationship, she assumed a different type of role with Joyce. Characteristic of many partnerships among couples in this study, this new level of relatedness included more equality in role behaviors. It was not easy for Joyce to adapt to the changes in her partner, as Joyce had to give up a role that, originally, had been satisfying to her and of value to both partners. The process of adapting to new relational realities took place over several years. Modifications in roles occurred inevitably as partners gradually changed specific interpersonal behaviors in their daily lives together. It was never a rapid process.

In some relationships, personal traits remained constant and resulted in reciprocal roles that did not change substantially, although there may have been specific behavioral modifications as relationships developed. Nancy and Nina, whose relationship has lasted twenty years, talked about the continuity in the structure of their roles. Nancy observed that:

> Our roles were and probably still are a little more blurred now, but are basically consistent with our personalities . . . being an inside person and an outside person. It was always my job to make the phone call, to arrange social plans, to arrange travel plans, to keep up the letter writing, to buy presents for family birthdays. I think the roles were more in that sense rather than a division of labor. In terms of the more traditional stuff, again, they go on our interests more than anything else. I do the cooking and Nina does everything else. She does the outside work and the laundry . . . she has always done that, taken care of the cars and that kind of thing.

Nina spoke of how their roles remained more rather than less constant, although circumstances in their lives changed. She observed that they define themselves "by the time we spent together," which raised the question of what changed and what did not change as these relationships developed. Based on how individuals talked about their relationships, it seemed that behavioral modifications came about without substantive change in other parts of the self. Those parts of the self appeared to have continuity over the years, which included a fundamental human need to be loved, characterological traits internalized from one's childhood and youth, and feelings about one's sense of personal worth. As partners made modifications in specific role behaviors, changes gradually occurred in one's inner needs and feelings. As a consequence, esteem for oneself, modes of defending against threats to one's psychological integrity, and emotional vulnerabilities associated with past experiences in relationships were modified. Such modifications came about by changes negotiated in relational roles and not by direct confrontation of defenses, traits, or needs. Those modifications were what adaptation was all about. By the continuity in role behaviors over the years, Nancy and Nina were adapting to life together in a way that accommodated their needs and personal traits. Most couples, such as Jennifer and Joyce, adapted by modifying relational behaviors.

The evolution of roles involved the dynamic interplay of past experiences with new realities. The process of change was never rapid or without pain. Felise spoke about the dynamic interplay of the past with the present in her relationship of nineteen years with Flora:

I came out of a marriage absolutely burned out, exhausted and angry, resentful. My husband and I worked long hours and I had a second job . . . he was extremely critical. . . . I just got madder and madder and madder. When he was unemployed, he did nothing. He just went helpless. . . . I grew up extraordinarily resentful of this. I had two brothers who had privileges that I didn't have. I watched my mother get exhausted and my grandmother virtually take care of a helpless husband. I just really wanted something different in my life, so when I got in a relationship with Flora, I just couldn't believe it. That was so wonderful! I was just so tired . . . pretty soon she began to do most of the marketing and the cooking. . . . I did the laundry and some of the cleaning. . . . We kind of had this evolution of interests. We just did the things that we like to do and what we were interested in doing . . . for a long time that felt fine to me but I started out with more expectations for what a home should be like than she did. I mean Flora would have no problem just sort of letting it all go. She knows what her priorities are . . . she has also had the kinds of jobs that have taken her away from the home most of the day and sometimes at night and a lot of traveling. I increasingly had a career where I have worked at home more. . . . I have just found myself more and more taking responsibility for the rest of our life except for the cooking and shopping. . . . I felt responsible for the house, and she felt responsible for her career. . . . I also felt responsible for my career. She would schedule her life, what needed to be done for her career . . . then she would work like a dog around the house with the time that she had. But what I didn't get was that I would be at home and I would be the default person. We sort of had this sliding that went on for years. I began to get very unhappy about it, but we couldn't seem to change it. . . . I never felt that I could complain because . . . she brought in more income and she made more money than I did. We just had a terrible time of it because both of us liked the money. So we just struggled with this reoccurring theme for a long time . . . it got better over the years . . . she's cut back on work . . . she has been doing all the things that didn't get done for years. I have a housewife; it is wonderful. I have been waiting all my life for this . . . now its completely flipped. . . . I am loving it . . . she is an extraordinarily hard worker. Both of us would work all those hours; it's just that we couldn't get the division right. We couldn't get it divided right . . . part of it is my struggle with my ambivalence with having to work and having to let go . . . we just have very different standards . . . each of us has evolved a little on this topic.

Before meeting Flora, Felise was caught in an unhappy marriage for several years. Her memories of that time suggest that she was replicating the roles her mother and grandmother had played in their marriages. In repeating this relational pattern in which she was subservient to her husband, Felise experienced increased feelings of frustration and felt powerless to change the relationship. Although much happier in her new relationship with Flora than she had been in the marriage, Felise only gradually became aware that similar inequities had crept into this relationship; she was repeating the intergenerational themes of role inequities based on gender differences that had plagued her in the past. She brought no other relational model to the partnership with Flora. As this relationship developed, Felise recognized the power she surrendered to Flora, the guilt she felt for her resentments, and the intergenerational themes of inequities in the relationships between women and men in her family. The perpetuation of these conflicts was reinforced by the inequality in the incomes of each partner. A catalyst for change in their roles was an employment change by Flora that reduced her income and required a realignment of household roles. Felise then experienced the inner feelings of fairness and equity that she hoped for when she met Flora.

Felise and Flora were able to negotiate a new balance in their relationship. An essential element in that shift was the willingness of each partner to accept responsibility for their behaviors. Mutually exploring the long-standing patterns of inequities in their relationship and accepting feelings associated with those patterns resulted in a new level of relatedness. The shift in roles seemed to have a positive effect on how each partner regarded herself, an aspect of change that was not only evident in the interview with Felise but also in the interview with Flora as she talked about modifications in their roles over the years. This couple illustrated that relational behaviors could change only when individuals were involved meaningfully in the process of negotiating roles and accepting the reality that one partner could not change unless the other one did. Among these couples, change in role behaviors was a mutual process.

A gay couple spoke about how their roles had changed and not changed since the beginning of the relationship seventeen years before our interview. Keith observed:

We fell into the roles that we still have, to some degree, today . . . we had no role models, and when friends would say: "Well who's the husband, who's the wife?" . . . it was like neither of us. I do more of the cooking because I enjoy it, and he does more of the social planning, because it comes naturally to him . . . there weren't defined roles . . . for years we resisted having sides of the bed, and we still don't have places at the table; we move around the table: "Where do you want me to sit?" "Well, wherever you want to sit." We would move from side to side and end to end daily . . . it's part of not wanting to have gender-specific, traditionally gender-specific roles, because that's not who we are; why should we re-create that? It sort of has to do with natural abilities is the way that I see it . . . my sister and I were talking about this the other day because we have very similar relationships with our partners in that we are nurturing to the point of creating invalids. We like to do everything, do all the cooking, do all the shopping, and if you don't watch us we'll do all the cleaning and we'll make everything just right, to the point of making the other person somewhat ineffective at running their own lives, because we are doing everything. The last five years have sort of been different because we've changed roles. Before that I traveled in my work . . . so I was not here; I was sort of absent for big chunks of time, and so he had a lot of running the household stuff . . . if anything was going to happen, he did it, and then I would come home from a trip and I would be like: "The house is a wreck" and all that stuff. When I moved into working from the house, we had a change of complexion because I'm here and it's easier to do stuff that I tend to do. I've always tended to do the bulk of the cooking, because I do it easier; I think of it as sort of occupational therapy, and I like to do it. We don't have defined chores. . . . I cook, so he cleans. If the phone rings he takes a call right after dinner, and I'll wash the dishes. There's a lot of flexibility . . . the last one out of bed makes the bed. It's not his job nor my job to do such and such. So that sort of goes back and forth.

His partner, Ken, talked of the importance of maintaining a balance in household tasks, especially in view of the shifts in their roles as a result of career changes. An important aspect in adapting to change was monitoring how a partner felt by "checking in on things regularly, just to make sure it doesn't become an issue . . . by talking about tasks and sort of what fit at various times."

Keith had a very nurturing personality that had the potential of creating a permanent caretaking role with Ken. However, both individuals had rejected rigid norms for structuring their relationship and valued flexibility in negotiating roles. The personality differences between them may have caused significant conflict. A method of coping with that possibility and of adapting to personal differences, which did not change, was monitoring how each partner felt about their behaviors in the relationship. It was not so much the number or the equitable division of tasks that was critical to them; rather, it was important that each partner contributed, in their own way, to the household. In that way, a balance was maintained in the relationship. One partner expressed concern about the continued balance in their relationship when the other partner took on greater household responsibilities. To make sure that the relationship remained stable, one partner had the responsibility of checking regularly with the other about the division of household chores. In general, gays spent less time than lesbians in discussing and processing their thoughts and feelings about equity in their relationships. The focus of gays was on balancing tasks and responsibilities according to each partner's interest, abilities, work schedules, and personal needs. For them, equilibrium rather than equity appeared to be the central issue in adapting to each other.

SUMMARY

The roles of gay and lesbian partners were explored from two perspectives: the qualities within themselves that came from models with whom individuals had identified and the shaping effect of reciprocal interactions between partners. Their voices suggested several sources on which roles were modeled. Parents were the most commonly reported role models; more than seven out of ten respondents reported that they were similar, in some respects, to at least one parent. Frequently mentioned similarities were a caring attitude toward one's partner, respect for that person, and love, support, and commitment to the relationship. Fewer than three out of ten respondents did not report similarities and felt that their relationships with partners were more open to communication, less conflictual, less abusive, and more equitable than the marriages of their parents. As a consequence, they rejected parents as role models and looked elsewhere for figures of identification on which to base their relationships.

In addition to or in spite of parental figures, gays and lesbians identified other models who were influential in developing their relational roles. Other gay and lesbian couples were mentioned by some individuals. When most of these people were struggling with matters of sexual orientation, lifestyle, and personal identity that characterized the transition from adolescence to early adulthood, values and norms for relationships were determined by the heterosexual world. Although some shifts in attitudes and social policies had occurred, there was still strong public sentiment against homosexual lifestyles, including gay and lesbian relationships. Individuals who witnessed and identified with the successes of same-sex relationships were reassured that they, too, could have a successful relationship.

Some individuals talked of how they had identified with other individuals in heterosexual relationships. The identification was with the qualities of these people, such as their kindness or commitment to a spouse, which partners admired and wished to emulate in their own relationships.

Approximately one out of four individuals in this study had been previously married. A previous marriage was often experienced as a benchmark in one's life against which to evaluate the quality of current relationships. Although several gays and lesbians commented on the similarities between previous marriages and current relationships with their partners, most individuals experienced the two relationships very differently. The quality of communication, feelings of interpersonal equity, and acceptance of one's sexual orientation, which had been submerged in their marriages, were mentioned quite often.

Several partners worked at building relationships without relying extensively on experiences with parents, friends, other homosexual partnerships, and previous marriages to develop their relationships. The rejection of role models required prolonged periods of negotiation to work out roles and to process differences associated with ambiguities in roles. These couples felt unencumbered by stereotypical expectations and exercised a sense of freedom to build relationships that met their individual needs. For the most part, they were satisfied with their efforts.

A mixture of expressive and instrumental behaviors characterized the relational roles of gays and lesbians; gays were more likely to be instrumental or task oriented and lesbians to be expressive or oriented to reflecting on relational experiences with partners. The nature of role relations between partners was shaped primarily by the talents and skills of partners and, secondarily, by other factors such as personal interests and employment schedules. Both gays and lesbians rejected rigid expectations about relational behaviors, especially those related to traditional gender stereotypes. Rather, they valued negotiating relational roles, which evolved from early to recent years. The evolution of roles was focused on modifications in specific behaviors rather than change in one's inner sense of self. Modifications in specific role behaviors did result in positive changes related to esteem for and peace with one's self. Adaptation in these lasting relationships meant that shifts in role behaviors needed to include both partners. For gays, the need was for balance in allocating relational tasks and responsibilities. Lesbians expressed, more than gays, the importance of reflecting upon their experiences together in order to develop mutual understanding and commitment to their relationships.

3

Relational Fit

She's the calm to my storm. She is the eye of my hurricane.

We are all familiar with committed relationships that fail because the partners were "incompatible." Irreconcilable differences are often cited as the reason for divorce in marriage. We assumed that differences were just as critical to the viability of these gay and lesbian relationships. To understand how these relationships lasted, we explored the interpersonal fit of partners that was determined by the reciprocity of roles. Fit was conceptualized along a continuum marked at one end by differences and at the other by similarities. If role behaviors, as reported by individual partners, were characterized by differences in talents, skills, needs, and traits, the fit was of a complementary nature. For example, if one partner was quiet and the other was outgoing, the fit was considered to be complementary. A symmetrical fit was characterized by similarities between partners. Most individuals used complementary language in describing their roles with their partners.

Patterns of complementarity between partners were similar over the years; 85 percent of lesbian and 75 percent of gay respondents described their roles as different from early to recent years. The complementary patterns of instrumental to expressive roles, the relational fit between partners, were remarkably consistent, although specific role behaviors changed as relationships developed. These modifications took place within a relational fit that did not change substantially for most respondents from early to recent years. For example, a quiet and submissive partner could become more expressive and assertive without a sweeping change in relational fit.

We found a different pattern in the relational fit between partners in their values. Most partners had similar beliefs, although their individual talents, skills, needs, and psychological traits differed. Values that included trust, respect, sensitivity, understanding, equity, and commitment offered meaning to relationships. Values also were the "glue" that helped to hold relationships together during stormy periods. A continuity in shared values between partners emerged during interviews as they spoke of their attitudes and beliefs about their relationships.

These two dimensions of relational fit had important functions in the process of adaptation over the years: complementarity enriched relationships and enabled individuals to experience a sense of wholeness. Symmetry in values had a containing function that allowed differences to be negotiated without undermining relationships.

COMPLEMENTARITY TO SYMMETRY

Claire and Candice, who have been together forty years, spoke of how perceived differences stimulated conflicts that were destructive if not negotiated successfully; their discussion illustrated how psychological differences, which were evident in the roles of each partner, had the function of enabling individuals to experience wholeness within themselves. Claire observed:

> Because of the family background that Candice had, or lack of it, as far as her parents being separated, I think that I became very nurturing. My role, though I may not have been able to tell you that then, was one of a nurturer and it has remained nurturing. . . . She's the calm to my storm. She is the eye of my hurricane. . . . I see myself as always overreacting, and being a flooder, and getting all worked up over everything . . . she is the one saying, it'll work out. She's the yin to my yang. . . . I have a certain way of doing things; I'm an obsessive-compulsive. Candice is not. She is very quiet, I'm more a talker. She is very laid-back. She sits there watching me, knowing sooner or later I'll settle down somewhere. I usually turn to her and I'll say: "What do you think?"

And she'll say: "Well, this is what I think." And I'll say: "Yeah, you're probably right!"

I once said to a friend: "She never asks me for anything." I always seem to need more. I'm always asking to change something. My friend said to me: "Your needs are different. She's just happy to have your presence felt, and you want more; you want dialogue, you want some kind of attention, you want to be doing something together, some kind of interaction, and not mindlessly doing something as a distraction. It's just that you have different needs." That made me feel better.

Claire commented on a common theme in the roles and relationships between partners. Psychological differences that had become part of each person had a powerful effect in shaping interpersonal behaviors. Individuals were attracted to potential partners who could offer them different types of experiences than they had in the past. For example, they looked for someone who would provide nurturing, acceptance, and love that may have been missing in other important relationships. Conversely, other individuals also looked for partners whom they could take care of and nurture. So-called needy individuals offered as much to their partners as they received. Many of these relationships were a vehicle to continue their personal development throughout adulthood.

Complementary differences were a catalyst for change toward a personal sense of wholeness within each partner. Differences also served to enhance the quality of their relationship. Developmental themes were evident as Claire talked of her role in the relationship with Candice. Claire was the explosive nurturer whose need to offer love was complemented by her partner's calmness. Claire and Candice found qualities in each other that they had not received in their families that enabled them to develop as individuals and as a couple. Personal and relational development were inseparable; one could not happen without the other.

As the friend of Claire observed, the needs of people come from past developmental experiences. Claire had been reared in a family that was highly expressive of emotions. Verbal interchanges were expected and valued. She had a need to continue this level of interaction; when it did not occur in the relationship with Candice, she began to wonder what she had done to cause this breach. Individuals who brought needs for this level of dialogue, along with needs to take care of partners, into relationships often experienced considerable remorse and guilt when their partners did not respond as they expected. This happened to Claire.

Candice reflected on the complementary nature of their relationship as she talked about Claire's qualities, which were experienced as fulfilling missing pieces within herself:

> We're very different people, which is probably what has kept us together. If I ever got involved with someone like me, we wouldn't have made it to the next month. I think that I'm there for her when she needs someone. . . . She goes crazy, makes mountains out of molehills all the time. She needs someone to calm her down and bring her back to reality. I think that the strength that I have, or that she thinks that I have, is something that attracted her to me. . . . She's a very nurturing person. She's always there, no matter what you need or what you've done. She's always there. I think that's the strength that she has that draws me to her. Her sense of humor. Her empathy. Her ability to bring out the best in me. She has an ability to make me look at myself and make me the kind of person I want to be. She gives me things that I've never had. That, probably more than anything else, keeps us together, as far as I'm concerned. What kept me in this relationship through all of the trials was a need that I had for someone to give me what I was lacking in my life. She never hesitated to be right there for me, to nurture or push me, to try to force me to grow as a person, whether I wanted to or not. As much as it annoyed me at times, I think, it's what helped me, over everything else. Basically, what kept us together was my own need for something that's lacking in my life.

Complementing the expressive and caretaking personality of Claire, Candice spoke about the other half of their relational equation. As her partner had observed, Candice was the "yin to my yang." She offered calmness to the storminess of Candice and a methodical approach to coping with life compared to her partner's impulsive style. There was a remarkable self-observing strength in the way she talked about the importance of complementary differences between them. Candice understood the personal assets and liabilities that each partner brought to the relationship and how their differences enabled each of them to grow within their relationship.

Claire and Candice expressed clearly how relationships were grounded on and held together by individual differences. The nurturer offered nurturing and, in turn, received fulfillment from her role. The stormy personality was calmed by the laid-back partner, a role that offered her meaning and importance in the relationship. Individuals, such as Claire and Candice, found qualities in each other that may have been insufficient or unavailable in developmental experiences in their families and with other primary figures. Relational differences were a catalyst for change. Such themes were very common in interviews as partners explored relational differences.

Along with being a catalyst and a resource for nurturing wholeness, differences also provided balance in relationships. The meaning of differences as providing relational balance was a prominent theme as Daniel and Dwight spoke of their differences throughout their seventeen-year relationship. Daniel observed:

> Dwight always thinks that he knows a solution to a problem or the answer to something; he's very self-confident . . . he's a powerful personality. I am also, but in very different ways. I can be very moody and I have very dark moods. And so we balance each other . . . he'll show me the lighter side of something when I'm thinking I want to hide under a rock . . . that's probably part of what's made it work; we have a lot of interests together, but we are very, very different. But that's a good balance . . . he's the optimist, and I'm the pessimist. He's the romantic. . . . I like dramas and he likes comedies.

The differences between the partners in this relationship were pronounced. They appeared to be polar opposites. The differences came from character traits that had a significant effect in shaping the complementary nature of their roles. Despite the big differences in several aspects of their relationship, they did have interests in common, such as friendships, travel, and food. No doubt, these similarities helped to maintain the connection between them. More important, however, was the symmetry in values, especially mutual commitment to the relationship, which provided a foundation on which to develop tolerance for their differences. Dwight offered his thoughts about relational differences and their significance to him:

> I'm the extrovert, the social one; he's the introvert, reading. He won't even answer the phone if I'm not home. He can be that introverted. . . . We've developed a lot of things in common. We love travel, good food, wine, movies, plays. We have things in common, but we have differences. It's not boring that way . . .

there's a balance. I couldn't live with someone too similar. Balancing each other out has been very important.

In addition to providing balance in the relationship of Daniel and Dwight, differences were a vehicle for keeping excitement in their lives, a theme mentioned by several respondents. Although differences may have enabled partners to experience a sense of wholeness and to feel excitement about being together, an inevitable consequence of complementarity in roles was conflict. The process of working out an acceptance of and tolerance for relational differences brought a renewed sense of stability as time passed. The qualities of openness, honesty, and acceptance of differences were crucial to the survival of these relationships.

TRUST AND RESPECT

Values, an integral component of relationships, infused roles with significance and meaning; they had a critical effect on how individuals thought and felt about themselves, their partners, and the quality of their relationships. A cluster of beliefs was explored; these relational values included trust, respect, sensitivity, understanding, equity, and commitment to the relationship. Values were explored from two perspectives: respondents trusting their partners and respondents feeling that their partners trusted them.

Compared to gays, lesbians were more trusting of their partners from early to recent years. The percentages of respondents saying that they trusted their partners increased through the years. The differences between gays and lesbians in their trust of partners were not substantial and may have reflected what this value meant to each group. When asked if they felt that their partners trusted them early in the relationship, more than seven out of ten individuals replied positively, a figure that was nearly the same for both groups. After a slight decline during the middle years in how individuals saw their partners trusting them, nine out of ten respondents from both groups responded positively during recent years.

Kate and Kristin talked about trust. Kate referred to the ambiguity of the word *trust*, which came up often in interviews. Trust, as Kate said, was a matter of sexual monogamy as well as a psychological component in relationships. Lesbians, more than gays, spoke explicitly about sexual fidelity as important to the quality of relationships. Of equal importance was the perception of one's partner as a good listener who accepted what one needed to talk about regardless of the subject. Kate described how trust changed as they "got to know each other"; she felt that they had grown in mutual trust, not only sexually but emotionally.

As Kristin talked of the meaning of trust to their relationship, we got a better understanding of why Kate appeared circumspect in talking about trust. For them, as for many other couples, trust needed to be nurtured in circumstances that tested the viability of relationships. Kristin described how trust unfolded between them. She referred to her personal history and the impact of developmental experiences on her capacity to trust anyone; also mentioned was the significance of a sexual affair on the relationship:

> We had gotten over this business of throwing me out. What she did do, which she had every right to do, and she had said right from the start: "You know, I'll never totally trust you the way I did before." That put a bit of a pall on things. I understood it both intellectually and emotionally, and felt: "OK, I can cope with that," but it was also very hard. I think one of the central things is the ability to talk things through, to talk things out, to share, to really be able to stop in the middle of what's going on when it gets crazy, and step back and see what's going on here. I don't want to sound simplistic because on the surface that makes eminent sense, but I also know that my ability to trust in that process did not come out of me but out of the relationship. I have taxed the relationship in many ways. . . . It went through a lot of tests and a lot of ups and downs in those first years.

Kristin then discussed the impact of her sexual affair on their relationship:

> I think she felt that her trust in me had been terribly violated when I got involved in the affair. I think we had to work really hard to restore that. After the first five or seven years, even though we had a lot of problems, it was never a trust issue. In fact, that was so entrenched and clearcut that I think that was one of the things that really helped us to do the other work we needed to do . . . we would always come back to the realization: we can trust each other. . . . Let's use that to listen, to look a little bit more carefully. I think that's been one of our greatest resources, and I don't feel that in the beginning we were wise enough to use it consciously.

Kristin described how trust was the basis of relationships. For her and others, mutuality of relational values was fundamental to the quality of relationships. She talked about difficulties in attaining and in maintaining mutual trust. According to Kristin, the ability to trust her partner was compromised by her earlier experiences in her family, which had left wounds that had not healed. Feelings that had been internalized as a result of those experiences undermined a capacity to trust people in general. Disclosure of the sexual affair precipitated a crisis that nearly fractured the connection between Kate and Kristin. Their commitment to each other enabled them to weather the storm of mistrust that extended over several years. In fact, it took more than five years before any significant healing occurred. As a result, Kate and Kristin reached a new level of mutual trust, which was the basis for building a relationship that has lasted more than twenty-five years. Finally, as Kristin points out, trust in each other enabled these partners to develop mutual empathy.

Although emotional trust was fundamental to the quality of these relationships, there was a difference between gays and lesbians in how monogamy was valued. Daniel commented on the importance of emotional trust:

> I've felt a lot of trust, and I would say that would probably be from the beginning. Because he was always there for me, whether it be . . . anything . . . my feeling uncomfortable with starting a new job, or needing to be propped up emotionally. . . . I never felt that he would betray me.

Dwight commented on how he viewed trust between them:

> I've always trusted that Daniel wouldn't do anything to hurt me . . . and that he'd be there for me when I needed him. Sometimes . . . well really until the last period, I have wondered if he might be seeing others.

Monogamy was valued differently by lesbians than it was by gays. For lesbians, trust was an inherent part of monogamy and sexual fidelity. Trust levels among gays were compromised by sex outside the relationship, but sex with others did not appear to have the same significance as in lesbian relationships. Although some sexual affairs were reported by lesbians, as it was by Kate and Kristin, sex with another person was rare among lesbians after a mutual commitment to the relationship had been made. Among gays, sex outside the relationship was common: 75 percent of gays compared to 25 percent of lesbians reported having sex with others after living with their partners. For gays, trust was as much a matter of emotional constancy of partners as it was a matter of sexual fidelity. Dwight made that point when he commented that his partner would be there when he needed him and would not do anything to hurt him. Several gays considered their partners trustworthy when partners provided constant emotional support despite their sexual affairs.

Mutuality of respect was another important value in maintaining relational stability. Only slight differences were found between lesbians and gays when they talked of how partners respected them and how they respected their partners; more than eight out of ten lesbians and seven out of ten gays reported mutual respect during the early years of their relationships, which increased only slightly during the middle years; in recent years, mutual respect was reported by more than nine out of ten respondents.

Although respect was high at the beginning of relationships, most respondents said that respect developed over time. That development was based on the personal qualities of individuals as well as their achievements in careers. As one gay partner observed: "Even after the beginning wore off, I think he has highly respected me as a person and for my work."

When there was a problem with respect, it was related to the behavior of an individual, which was often symptomatic of a personal problem. If a partner avoided taking responsibility for doing something about the problem, or if attempts to overcome the problem were unsuccessful, that behavior tended to breed disrespect, as in the following relationship. Gary expressed how the respect of his partner for him was contingent on Gary's commitment to master an addiction. Talk was not enough to gain respect; it needed to be earned through responsible behavior. Kristin had expressed a similar value about the development of respect in her relationship with Kate. Gary said:

> I have a tremendous amount of respect for him. . . . Early on a tremendous amount of respect . . . before I got sober, which was part of the third phase, he showed a tremendous amount of disrespect toward me. . . . I didn't use the word "respect" but I did use the word "regard" many times. I said: "When I feel that you show some regard for me, I will return that; it will come right back to you. But you have disregard for me right now.". . .

> George can be very, very critical. . . . I said: "I'm going to take
> the alcohol and the drugs away, and we'll see where we're at."
> And it turned around . . . he gained a tremendous amount of
> respect for me.

His partner, George, described the rocky road that both traveled
throughout their sixteen-year relationship to reach a level of mutual
respect:

> My respect for Gary has come completely full circle. No respect
> in the second phase . . . now I've never respected anybody more
> in my life. He is an unbelievable man. He's a guy that if he's going
> to do something, he does it, whether it be to stop smoking and
> drugging. . . . I can only aspire to being more like him. The
> beginning phase, respect, nothing all that great. Getting to know
> each other, getting to know our moral, my business ethics, and
> things like that. Second phase, Gary lost all respect for me. . . .
> I wasn't respecting him all that much because of things I was
> feeling . . . right now, Gary respects me . . . he has new respect
> for my work ethics. On a personal level, I think he has a lot of
> respect for me.

Although the road to mutual respect may have been more difficult
for this couple than for others, their story illustrated how fundamental
trust and respect were to the quality of relationships. The story also
depicted how respect evolved through the years. For some couples, the
evolution of respect included dramatic changes in behavior that were
"worthy" of admiration. For most couples, mutual respect that began
at a high level did not change appreciably but was strengthened through
the years.

UNDERSTANDING AND SENSITIVITY

There were separate questions about understanding and sensitivity.
As with trust and respect, we asked how understanding and sensitive
respondents were toward their partners as well as how understanding
and sensitive respondents perceived their partners to be toward them.
In that way, we were able to assess the mutuality of these relational
values. There were differences in the patterns of understanding and
sensitivity as relationships evolved.

During the early years of relationships, gays viewed themselves as
more understanding of their partners than did lesbians toward their

partners. Almost six out of ten gays compared to slightly more than three out of ten lesbians described themselves in that way. Lesbians were more likely to use mixed language in recalling their understanding of partners during those years; that is, more than half of lesbian respondents said that they were not very understanding toward their partners during the early years, at least not as understanding as they were at the present time. Among lesbians, understanding of partners developed steadily over the years; by the current phase, nine out of ten lesbians compared to eight out of ten gays saw themselves as understanding of their partners. When we asked how understanding respondents felt their partners were toward them, the responses were quite different: about half of all respondents experienced their partners as understanding of them during the early years; in recent years, more than eight out of ten individuals, more lesbians than gays, felt that their partners were understanding of them.

The way in which mutual understanding developed between lesbian partners was evident in excerpts from an interview with Abby as she talked about their relationship, which has lasted twenty years:

> She has a lot of understanding of what's going on, and she can sometimes see things before I do . . . she can see this is too stressful or we really can't do this. . . . I think in the beginning there was not a lot of understanding of what I was going through and there was not a lot of understanding of what she was going through; I mean, there was just no understanding . . . it was in the middle period; there was a lot of negotiation, and I think that it was fairly mutual.

The development of mutual understanding was tied intimately to the development of a sense of "bonding" between partners. Mutuality in understanding could not be experienced outside of a meaningful connection, nor could a relational bond be sustained without understanding. The following excerpt portrayed the interdependence of these two central ingredients for development of relationships. The process involved a deepening level of personal disclosure with another human being on whom one could depend as a safe ally. For the couple in this example, the disclosure involved past sexual abuse of one partner, which had plagued her for years with questions of personal adequacy and mistrust of others. For the other partner and for most other individuals, the process involved a growing comfort in allowing one's inner self to emerge in the relationship. Abby continues:

So it's changed, to now a much better understanding with each other . . . I think that was part of what our initial bonding was about, it was about understanding. I think that on a more practical level, her understanding of me has come out of the degree of my ability to come out of my interiorness and give her something to understand. That has been a process. . . . My understanding of her, I think, is an important thing . . . there were times when I could say I didn't understand why she would do what she did. I had a hard time understanding how someone with as much intelligence and education and sort of everything going for her, why she would get stuck in places that required some self-assurance or assertiveness. Why she would be fearful at times . . . it wasn't until after she burst forth with her abuse history that I have been really able to understand some of the stuff I couldn't before. Prior to her claiming those memories, I really have to say, I couldn't understand why she was as timid or skittish as she was. . . . It's not that I didn't love her, but I honestly couldn't understand some things. Neither could she, for that matter. But so many things have come into perspective since those memories and the healing process she has done. So much has become so much clearer.

Abby's partner, Alicia, talked about the development of mutual understanding in their relationship, which was achieved after a long and, at times, difficult process. The route toward mutual understanding was through couples psychotherapy through which partners became increasingly able to tell each other their inner thoughts and feelings. Alicia commented on how therapy helped her and Abby to develop mutual understanding:

I think we have great understanding of each other. We look at our relationship and talk about it. I think she understands me quite well, and I think I understand her quite well . . . when you first get to know someone, you don't understand them that much. I guess I would go back to the time when we were doing couples therapy where we both grew to understand ourselves and each other a lot. We were trying to understand each other, but we didn't have the tools to do it.

Both partners had become stalled in their efforts to understand each other. Like many couples, they entered treatment to understand what was preventing them from having a relationship that both wanted. Therapy provided a format to help them communicate their needs, which enabled them to become unstuck and to move ahead on the road to mutual understanding.

Sensitivity referred to the emotional aspect of understanding; understanding, as we have discussed it, was a cognitive process. To be sensitive was to be attuned emotionally to the feeling state of the partner. One could be sensitive without understanding all of the dynamics, now and in the past, that contributed to a problem the partner was experiencing. To be sensitive was to acknowledge and to accept the feelings of the partner without necessarily understanding them.

A higher percentage of lesbians compared to gays viewed themselves as sensitive toward their partners throughout the years. In contrast to the perceptions of one's sensitivity toward a partner, almost two out of three individuals experienced their partners as sensitive to them during the early and middle years of their relationships.

Abby described the process of becoming sensitive when she observed that "in the earlier and middle years . . . if I sensed that she was angry . . . I wanted to fix it or I felt I could do something to make her better as opposed to now being sensitive to her moods and saying: 'Do you want to talk about it? Do you want to be alone? Do you want me to hold you ?'" She went on to say: "I've changed from wanting to fix it to now just allowing it. . . . Acknowledging that she is in a funk and that's fine, or what she wanted to do to get out of it or if I can be of help or if not, fine. It's more okay with me how she feels than it used to be."

Mutual empathy has been identified as a characteristic of mature relationships between women. Empathy was a form of sensitivity that evolved through the years as lesbian partners worked on deepening their understanding of each other. Abby was sensitive to her partner's needs in the early years but could not separate her own needs from those of her partner. Gradually she developed the skill to be with her partner and yet to respect that person's boundaries. Rather than act on her sense of the partner's state, she began to ask for permission to comfort her. She no longer needed to rescue her partner. She was able to contain those needs and be with her partner in the way that was responsive to the partner's needs rather than to her own needs. When partners reached that point in the development of their relationships, they were making a transition from being sensitive to being empathic.

Abby went on to describe her partner as "inordinately sensitive to me, she is a feeler. Sometimes she senses things about me . . . she is almost always aware of where I am at." Finally, she commented on the differences between her and her partner: "I am not by nature a feeling kind of person; I cannot be sensitive initially. I am a thinking type of person, so I feel that at times I am not as sensitive to her needs. . . . She anticipates my needs; I don't anticipate hers. Once I am aware of her needs, then I think I am reasonably sensitive to them." Abby identified an important aspect in the development of relationships: differences compromised movement toward genuine mutuality only when they were ignored or not faced honestly. If partners were unable to let the other partner know of their needs, the likelihood of moving toward mutual empathy was undermined.

Relational values of trust, respect, understanding, and sensitivity enriched these relationships. Differences were found between gays and lesbians in the meaning and significance of trust. Compared to lesbians, gays tended to make distinctions between sexual fidelity and emotional availability; being able to count on a partner's availability as a loyal friend was more important than sexual monogamy. For lesbians, monogamy was a part of having a trustful relationship once a commitment had been made to each other. Values of mutual respect and under-standing were similar for gays and lesbians throughout their relation-ships. Lesbians seemed to value emotional sensitivity differently than gays. Sensitivity among lesbians was part of their investment in reflect-ing upon their relationships and being mutually attuned to each other.

The variations in how lesbians and gays discussed sensitivity and understanding in relationships appeared to reflect gender differences rather than their sexual orientations. Women may have been more comfortable than men in being with their partners even when they did not understand what was going on between them. Men may have been comfortable when they understood what was going on and were uncomfortable with aspects of relationships that they could not under-stand and control. Even the words *understanding* and *sensitivity* may have triggered different responses to our questions. Thus these men may have needed to see themselves as understanding from the begin-ning of relationships in order to feel a sense of control, while women could acknowledge the lack of understanding early in relationships. Lesbians appeared to be more adept than gays at accepting the ambi-guities of being in a relationship in which each partner was working toward mutual empathy. They viewed themselves as more sensitive than did gays. Sensitivity involved ambiguities about which men may have been more uncomfortable than were women. These qualitative differ-ences in relational values and how gay and lesbian partners dealt with them were similar to differences that have been found between men and women in other research.

EQUITY

Equity was defined as the sense of fairness that individuals experienced about their relationships as a whole. For most respondents, it was important for tasks and responsibilities to be allocated fairly for them to feel that relationships were equitable. In order to understand fairness, we explored several dimensions of relational fit by asking respondents to tell us how differences were balanced as they and their partners negotiated responsibilities for household tasks, handling money, and several other aspects of working out the day-to-day realities of living together. Relational fit was considered fair by most partners from the beginning years to the present time. Except during the middle years, gays and lesbians were quite close in their assessments of overall fairness. During the middle years, gays experienced a dip in their sense of fairness about relationships: 58 percent of gays compared to 73 percent of lesbians experienced their relationships as equitable. Lesbian partners worked to achieve a sense of fairness by maintaining open channels of communication between them. During the middle years, communication between gay partners deteriorated, and that may have contributed to the decline in equity.

Given the high levels of complementarity in these relationships, it was no surprise that equity became an important issue between partners. In contrast to similarities, differences meant that partners were not equal in what they brought to relationships. As a consequence, balances needed to be worked out in roles if fairness was to be realized. Isabelle and Ingrid spoke of how they struggled with differences to achieve a sense of fairness in their relationship that has lasted eighteen years. Isabelle talked about the influence of different personality types and unequal financial resources:

> Ingrid carries much more of the financial burden. That's certainly unequal, but I think that there are other ways that things balance out. . . . I can be more verbal and mouthy, so I have to be careful not to be too much, because I can probably dominate. . . . I don't feel like there's an unfairness. It's pretty balanced. One might have more than another at one point, but it balances out . . . early on, when we weren't really talking as much, there was not as much of a negotiation. If I was going to buy something, it didn't matter

what Ingrid thought . . . the more we talk, the more we communicate, it probably is more balanced.

Isabelle talked about various aspects of their relationship in which there were differences. There was an inequality in their incomes, so her partner carried more of the "financial burden." That inequity was offset by the strengths of Isabelle who, compared to Ingrid, was adept in expressing how she felt about relational issues. She considered that her skill in expressing feelings was an asset to the relationship that helped to balance the differences in incomes. For this couple and for others, economic and personal differences were realities that did not change to any substantial extent. The key to achieving a sense of fairness about their lives together was to work toward being able to talk honestly about differences. As communication improved, so did the sense of fairness about relationships.

From Ingrid's perspective, their struggles to find a balance and to achieve equity in their relationship were depicted as follows:

> I was the older one, I made more money, and it was unbalanced for a long time and not really talked about. I don't think I recognized it as being out of balance for a while. I would say I was the responsible one . . . not that Isabelle was irresponsible, but I just sort of took the responsibility . . . that's an issue we've struggled with. I finally recognized that's not what I wanted. Isabelle recognized that probably it wasn't what she wanted, but it's something, I think, we've had to work at. . . . I'm a little more task oriented than Isabelle just in sort of activities of daily living. It was easy for me to do the cleaning and all of that because I didn't necessarily have other things that I did with my time to the extent that she did . . . we continue to struggle with that sometimes, to try to keep that in a balance that works for each of us . . . so there are times when I'll feel overwhelmed, and there are times when it comes up for her. One of the things that's true about that division of responsibilities is I probably get more things done more quickly, but Isabelle probably does the task better . . . when she cleaned, it would be better than I'd do it . . . it's been important to us for it to be balanced . . . sometimes money can be an influence. We each have difficulty with the money. . . . I have more money, so I have more of the power, but sometimes her lack of resources makes me feel powerless because we can't do something that I want to do . . . we're sort of held back.

As Isabelle and Ingrid understood, equity was related to resources that each partner brought to the relationship. Financial resources were associated with power so that the more money one made, the more power one may have had in deciding relational issues. Conversely, Ingrid commented on how feelings of powerlessness could be triggered by a partner with lower income. In a real sense, it was easier to "measure" money as a source of power than it was to measure intangible resources that contributed to the quality of relationships. The challenge was in recognizing the value of different resources that partners brought to relationships. A sense of fairness was integrated into relationships as negotiations to work out household tasks, roles, and responsibilities were successful. Those negotiations were contingent on the development of effective communication between partners. Communicating about the significance of various resources and assigning a value to them were important aspects in achieving a fair balance in these relationships.

Another couple, Harriet and Hillary, who have been together twenty years, described the process of working toward fairness from the beginning of their relationship to the current time. Because of parity in incomes, negotiating a sense of relational equity was focused on other matters. Harriet reported:

> Early on I felt like I had to be responsible . . . it was not so much butch, as I felt somebody had to make the decisions, and I was willing to make the decisions. . . . Hillary was willing to go along with it because we didn't really disagree . . . it seemed like I got my way more. . . . I think we really struggled about those things in the middle and, in the past eight/nine years, we have negotiated more explicitly. But I don't think it's been unfair in any of those periods of time. . . . We have the same order of magnitude of income; we have the same order of magnitude at work.

Hillary described the process of negotiating a sense of fairness in the relationship:

> I think that each of us kind of perceives the other one as being more generous. I mean, I think that part of what allows you to keep your relationship going is to give more than what you see as 50 percent . . . it balances in the end, although I know that I give more than she does, and she knows she gives more than I do . . . we both gave less in the middle and more at the end and

> beginning, or maybe it just didn't seem like giving in the begin-
> ning; it just seemed: "Who cares?" . . . It didn't seem like
> compromise . . . you didn't even bother to disagree about things
> because it was so fresh. But in the middle we just clashed a lot.
> Now we both give much more than the other does.

The dynamics at play in reaching for equity in the relationship of
Harriet and Hillary were quite different from those of Isabelle and
Ingrid. Harriet spoke of her need to take responsibility early in the
relationship for making decisions, which was connected to issues of
power and control. She was the dominant personality who got her way
more often than Hillary. Both partners felt increasingly unhappy with
the imbalance in the relationship, which continued for many years.
Hillary's passivity gave way to a more assertive way of handling her
needs. The couple then had to negotiate a new level of relatedness based
on acceptance of differences and compromise. Relational balance was
nurtured in the later years by the belief that each partner gave more
than was necessary for the well-being of the other partner. Despite the
long conflictual process over achieving balance, these partners felt that
the relationship was fair to each of them over the years. As with other
couples, balances based on differences in talents, skills, personal traits,
status in careers, and income were part of the equation in reaching for
and in working toward relational equity.

COMMITMENT

All these couples were committed to each other. For most couples,
commitment signified a pledge of love and the dream of spending one's
life with their partner. As respondents talked about that pledge and
their dreams, they sounded like the couples in our earlier studies of
lasting marriages. Commitment involved an initial decision to be
faithful to the partner as well as an ongoing renewal of that pledge.
Although there were no social markers that signified the commitment
of these couples, such as a wedding ceremony, respondents identified
various happenings that marked their commitments. These happenings
included the decision to live together, being sexually intimate for the
first time, and buying joint property.

Jeffrey spoke about what commitment meant to his partner and to
him:

> Well, we've always considered ourselves to be married. I have a ring . . . a monogamous thing, like husband and wife. . . . We joined our lives together in every way possible. Our finances have always been commingled . . . we've always had joint accounts. Everything that we've purchased is in both names . . . everything that we do is always with regard to the other person. It's very important . . . maybe I want to do something Jason doesn't want to do, so I won't do it. Jason does the same thing with me, because he feels that the commitment is to make each other happy.

Jason mirrored how Jeffrey valued commitment:

> We understand it was for better or for worse, sickness and in health. I mean, there was no actual ceremony. We felt that way toward each other . . . there are rules and regulations and everything . . . when we went into the relationship it was to commit to each other, to love each other, to be with each other. It was just we wanted a home . . . we wanted a home together. We wanted family. I looked at it as a marriage.

Both Jeffrey and Jason, who have been together twenty-five years, valued their commitment in a similar way. Their comments sounded like any two people who loved each other enough to make a commitment to a relationship. This couple's commitment included sexual monogamy. Similar to this couple, aspirations for relational stability and a home were mentioned frequently by other partners.

Another form of commitment, mentioned with less frequency, focused on remaining together so long as the relationship served to facilitate the psychological and social development of each partner. For many of these couples, commitment had an important spiritual significance. The following couple, together for twenty-three years, described how their commitment to each other was intertwined with their spiritual journey. Beatrice said:

> I think we both felt that our commitment to try to live our lives as we best understood was basic for us and still is. That has been the most underlying foundation of our relationship. . . . We never made vows to each other in public. We kind of negotiated an ongoing commitment. . . . Maybe you can't vow for life. That is something we both struggled with a lot . . . really working through to a different understanding to what it is to make a commitment. . . . I said: "OK, God, this is who I am. When I deny it I get very

brittle and very critical and don't like who I am. This may be all
wrong, but this is who I am and I have to be honest with you if
you want to show me this is wrong." I was terrified and literally I
waited for the lightning bolt to strike me dead, that is how dead
it was. In retrospect now, what I have come to know about myself
that I didn't know about myself then was that I had experienced
a tremendous amount of abuse in my family of origin; sexual,
physical, and emotional. So my idea about God was very, very
colored by that. My father was not a loving, nurturing father. Bit
by bit the lightning bolt did not come. I started to meet other
Christians who were just as committed as I was and for whom this
was not a big issue. As I came to terms with that, other levels of
commitment could fall into place. I was very afraid of commitment.

Beatrice spoke of the struggle and pain to come to terms with her
sexuality, which had a significant effect on her reluctance to enter a
committed lesbian relationship. The process was complicated by an
abusive family history that had left its scars. Guilt about homosexuality
led to denial of a central part of herself and undermined any movement
toward relational commitment with another woman. The fear of being
exploited again, as she had been in her family, would not allow her to
become involved in an intimate relationship in which she felt vulnerable. She was plagued with guilt and, no doubt, a considerable amount
of shame for who she had been and for who she now was.

One cannot underestimate the importance of social supports from
peers, which helped many people to strive toward a sense of peace with
their sexuality. Other lesbians and gays, who shared her Christian
beliefs, enabled Beatrice to move beyond her guilt and shame and to
integrate a "different" sexual orientation into herself. Through these
social supports and in collaboration with her partner, Beatrice worked
persistently to accept herself as a whole person. In recent years, she was
experiencing a peace that had previously eluded her. While married,
Barbara recalled the instantaneous attraction she experienced to Beatrice:

I just liked her, and it just clicked. It was as though we had always
known each other. . . . I think that we were committed in the
beginning. We talked about it in terms of being committed. We
didn't have a clue what that would mean or what that would look
like. It was verbalized in different ways as time went on. . . . I
understood inwardly that this was the person I was meant to be
with. I didn't know what I was going to do with my own

homophobia or accept what I was. . . . I don't remember renegotiating that commitment very much. It was there; we talked about it as something that was there. Our struggle was what was that going to look like and how we were going to honor that. . . . I remember at some point along the line, we talked about how we might celebrate our relationship or symbolize it. Beatrice had wanted us to have rings, and I was hesitant about that. She wanted some kind of a ceremony . . . everytime we talked about this, I would balk and balk. I finally realized that what I was balking at was making ever again another vow for life . . . after having made one and having not been able to keep it, I could not do that again. What I learned is that I could never again promise to love someone until I die. Or, promise to stay with someone until they die; I can't make that kind of a promise. I have experienced the fact that life happens in the midst of your promises, and there they go . . . what I would rather be about was being committed to one another for as long as we were growing, for as long as we were enabling one another to be all that we could be and was good for the both of us. For me, that was the commitment.

Barbara had not been happy in her marriage for several years. The connection to Beatrice was complicated by her marriage as well as by the responsibility of being a mother. In addition to these realities, she was struggling, like Beatrice, to overcome homophobia and to accept herself as a lesbian. She "knew" what she wanted, a committed relationship with Beatrice, but could not figure out how they could be together. Her marriage vows influenced the type of commitment she was able to make to Beatrice. Barbara observed that she "could never again promise to love and to stay with someone until they die." Although the experiences of these two women, which shaped their values toward a committed relationship, were quite different, they arrived developmentally at a similar spot. Each partner was "prepared" to commit to a relationship so long as it supported their psychological, spiritual, and social development. They have been together for more than twenty years.

SUMMARY

Role differences had the complementary function of enabling partners to experience a sense of wholeness within themselves, to provide relationships with balances so that tasks were accomplished equitably, and to keep excitement alive, especially after partners had been together for several years. More than three out of four partners used complementary language in describing their relationships from the beginning years to the present time.

Behind these behavioral differences were values about relatedness between partners, which had a symmetrical quality to them. Values—trust, respect, sensitivity, understanding, equity, and commitment—gave meaning to roles and affirmed the centrality of these relationships in their lives. While differences had an adaptive function in these relationships, they had the potential to produce conflicts that could seriously damage and even destroy the connections between partners. Mutuality in these values prevented differences from having those effects.

For the most part, there was a mutuality of values between partners as well as a similarity in values between gays and lesbians. Differences were apparent between gays and lesbians in how they valued sensitivity and understanding. Lesbians perceived themselves as sensitive, and gays as understanding, particularly during the early years of relationships. These differences were likely related to how men and women valued being sensitive or being understanding. Gays may have needed to see themselves as understanding in order to have a sense of control in relationships. Lesbians seemed to value and to be tolerant of the ambiguities of being with their partners without necessarily having to understand what was going on between them. Lesbians valued the experience of processing experiences with their partners with the goal of enhancing the connections between them. Although this was true for gays, lesbians were particularly adept at reflecting upon their relational experiences and learning from these reflections.

The value of trust was also framed differently by gay and lesbian partners. For lesbians, trust was a matter of psychological availability and sexual monogamy. For most gays, trust did not include monogamy. Twenty-five percent of gays and 75 percent of lesbians said that they were sexually monogamous. Despite that difference, both gays and lesbians trusted their partners to be available to them when they needed an accepting, supportive, and caring listener, someone to whom they could turn without feeling threatened.

The sense of fairness about relationships was shaped by several factors. Differences in income were a source of inequity, especially among lesbian couples. For lesbians to feel a sense of fairness about being together, material and nonmaterial resources that partners contributed to and took from relationships needed to be perceived as balanced. Equity was a value that appeared more important to the well-being of lesbian relationships than of gay relationships. For lesbians, much time was invested in processing differences that often reflected the importance of preserving individual autonomy within a meaningful relationship. Gays talked less about negotiating matters that stimulated feelings of unfairness. They attributed fairness to a fifty-fifty partnership, which gay partners thought characterized their relationships over the years. In both gay and lesbian relationships, differences were balanced by the mutual recognition and acceptance of resources that each partner contributed to relationships.

Commitment to most relationships was an affirmation of loyalty to the partner. For many couples, commitment was framed as a pledge to remain in the relationship as long as it served as a positive resource in the psychological, social, and spiritual development of each partner.

4

Decision Making

I have a tendency inside myself to run decisions into the ground with anxiety. She can be very direct.

In a relationship, decisions are made about scores of matters from the sublime to the mundane. Some decisions, such as a major purchase, may require deliberate and systematic thought before an actual decision is made. Decisions about modifying relational behaviors may occur incrementally between individuals over a long span of time. Gay and lesbian couples made decisions about many issues, including their roles, having or not having children, and the handling of money.

COMMUNICATION OVER TIME

Communication was a thread that connected partners and a vehicle for making decisions. The quality of communication, how effective individuals were in expressing their thoughts and feelings as well as listening to those of their partners, was a vital dimension of these relationships. Positive or effective communication was characterized by a sense of mutuality in which partners felt they could be honest about expressing their thoughts and feelings to each other and that their points of view would be accepted and respected even if the other partner disagreed with them. This chapter begins with a discussion of the quality of communication between partners. Four aspects of decision making are then examined: the changes in styles of decision making over time, negotiation of roles, decisions about having children, and decision making about finances.

The patterns of positive communication over the years are shown in figure 4.1. About half of respondents talked of their communication as being positive during the early years of their relationships. After partners had been together for a few years, the quality of communication remained the same between lesbians but regressed considerably among gays; positive communication was then reported by only 21 percent of gays. In order to determine if the regression among gay couples was a shared perception between partners, we examined the reports of each partner. Both partners in gay relationships reported similar observations about the deterioration in communication. In recent years, the quality of communication was described as positive by 85 percent of lesbians and by 54 percent of gays.

Differences in the quality of communication between lesbians and gays, particularly during the middle and recent years, was influenced by several factors. We have already discussed how gender differences appeared to be related to other dimensions of relationships including

Figure 4.1
Positive Communication between Partners

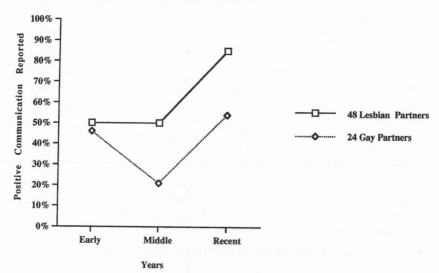

understanding and sensitivity. Differences in communication may also have been a manifestation of gender differences. More lesbian than gay couples appeared to have a high level of personal investment in reflecting on developments in their relationships. To be successful, that process required effective skills in expressing one's thoughts and feelings as well as listening to those of the partner. Lesbians appeared to be more adept than gays at processing their experiences and, as a consequence, the quality of their communication was better. An important part of processing was the valuing of mutual sensitivity and equity, which supported the development of interpersonal connections within lesbian relationships.

Another factor in the decline of quality in communication in gay relationships may have been related to the sexual affairs of several partners, which occurred after they had been together for a few years. Sexual affairs happened in the context of other conflicts between partners, which may have led to an erosion in the quality of their communication during the middle years. George commented on the deterioration in their relationship after five years of being together:

> The second five years things changed . . . communication broke down; I was unhappy; he was miserable; he was getting high; I was rejected, and all this foolishness. . . . I couldn't talk to him. . . . I cheated . . . he was busy doing other things, and he couldn't talk to me because I was so angry.

We cannot be sure to what extent sexual affairs had a negative effect on gay relationships in the middle years. There is no doubt that sex outside of relationships contributed to the decline in the quality of communication among some gay couples during that time. Many gays did not make an explicit connection about the effects of sexual affairs on regression in communication but did describe how angry, jealous, and hurt they were about their partners having sex outside their relationships. Usually several factors contributed to their unhappiness and, as a consequence, to difficulties with communication. In the interview, George spoke to how intertwined these factors were in relationships. In talking about the deterioration in their communication, which mingled with difficulties in their relationship in the middle years, Gary was upset with George's passive-aggressive behavior:

> One thing that has driven me absolutely crazy about George over the years is that he will "yes" me. He "yesses" me . . . and then

he goes ahead and does what he wants. I tell him: "I would rather you be more honest with me" . . . a lot of times I will walk away . . . he hands me a lot, and sometimes I would rather he didn't but I take responsibility for a lot . . . now, when I look back, I realize how silly it was.

Communication improved between gay partners in recent years, a theme evident in the observations of half of gay respondents. This was true for Gary and George. For the other half of gay respondents, communication remained a problem throughout their relationships; they talked of difficulties in expressing their thoughts and in maintaining a mutual level of openness with their partners. Henry spoke of that difficulty in his twenty-five-year relationship with Howard:

I don't think the communication is that great between us, verbal communication. . . . It's never been that great . . . he's harder to talk to than I am. . . . It's hard for me sometimes to carry on a conversation with him. . . . Sometimes he's just too agreeable. I can't find out what he really wants . . . his main thing is he really wants to please me. He wants to find out what I want, and I'm trying to find out what he wants . . . we don't really meet on that. . . . I always wished we could communicate better. I still do. I don't think it's all him, it's probably me too . . . we don't seem to be able to address the issue between us.

From the perspective of Howard, their difficulties with communication looked like this:

Well he doesn't think I talk much. . . . Henry's a talker. I'm not. In the evening time, I'm tired and I don't want to do anything after work, when I open that door. . . . But Henry's ready to go. He's ready to go out that door to dinner or some social thing. He's been home all day. I've been gone all day. I want to unwind; I want to take a shower; I might want a drink . . . if we have a spat, he wants to talk about it, but when we start talking about it, he gets upset. He runs upstairs and closes the door. If he doesn't come back in about a half hour, I'll go up and say: "What's your problem?" And he gets mad. He's a very serious person.

The dynamics that contributed to communication difficulties between gay partners did not appear to be different from those between lesbian partners. Yet gays had more problems in closing the fissures between them. That ongoing problem was evident in what Henry and Howard said about their relationship. Because of their investment in working on improving relationships and their skill in processing relational experiences, lesbian partners had more success in closing the gaps between them. Many lesbians described how they accomplished those changes. Deirdre talked about the process of working toward effective communication with Daphne, her partner for twenty-five years:

> I thought I did a lot of talking, but I didn't talk very much myself about my own feelings. I didn't know how to do that. I didn't have a model for doing that. My parents never did. . . . There wasn't real, honest, open communication until maybe five years ago. When I think of the way we communicate now, I'm calling it open and honest. I may have thought that was what we were doing back then. . . . I still have trouble with communication. I think that my mother really did a hell of a job on me. I know how important it is and I want to, so it is a struggle.

Deirdre, similar to many lesbian respondents, spoke of how partners dealt with communication difficulties. When communication improved between gay partners, they tended not to elaborate on the process through which changes were accomplished. Lesbians were more expressive than gays in describing how behavioral modifications had transpired and what they had learned about their relationships and themselves from processing experiences. As with Deirdre, lesbians seemed to have more comfort than did gays in reflecting on how their family backgrounds affected their capacity to be open with their partners, how they may have avoided closeness in relationships, and how they had made progress in communicating with their partners, despite chronic fears about abandonment.

Daphne spoke to the important distinction between talking and communicating and how she and Deirdre learned to listen to each other:

> We have attempted to communicate from the beginning. . . . I think what we have done is that we have learned how to communicate. Neither one of us felt heard or seen by the other. We didn't feel understood, and so then we learned how to communicate better. We learned how to talk better, we learned how to say what we needed or wanted. We both learned how to

listen better, get that other stuff out of the way so we could do
that. We've always tried, we just weren't successful at it.

Both gay and lesbian partners reported improvements in the quality
of communication in recent years. The route each group took in
arriving at the current state of their relationships was quite different.
Gays experienced significant regression in the quality of communication during the middle years, while the quality of communication
between lesbian partners remained about the same as it was in the early
years. Compared to gays, a higher percentage of lesbians reported
effective communication with their partners in recent years. The personal investment and skill in processing relational experiences and in
learning from them were evident in the observations of lesbian respondents. As in the previous discussion of roles and relational fit, these
findings suggested that gender differences played an influential role in
shaping the quality of communication between partners.

DECISION-MAKING STYLES

Before exploring decision-making styles of couples, we asked how
each respondent made decisions. Their individual approaches were
categorized as logical, impulsive, or intuitive, depending on the predominant way in which each respondent described themselves. Logical
decision makers considered the advantages and disadvantages of their
choices, which were made after a careful consideration of possible
outcomes. The impulsive style fell at the other end of the continuum;
these individuals acted quickly, with little or no thought about their
decisions. The intuitive style was defined as a reliance on an inner sense
or "gut feeling" rather than logic or reason. Intuitive decision makers
were confident about their skills.

The individual approach to making decisions among the majority of
gays and lesbians was to think through the pros and cons of a decision
before making a judgment. Lesbians were more likely to use such an
approach. Slightly more than half of gays and almost three-quarters of
lesbians described themselves as logical decision makers, percentages
that did not change appreciably from the early through recent years.
Those gays who did not describe themselves as logical decision makers
were split fairly evenly between impulsive and intuitive styles. Approximately 25 percent of gays compared to 10 percent of lesbians described
themselves as intuitive in making decisions.

With individual decision-making styles as a backdrop, we explored how couples went about making decisions. We focused on a wide range of issues about which couples communicated and made decisions, including negotiating roles, deciding to have or not have children, and handling finances. Respondents were also asked to describe how they and their partners went about making decisions as a couple from early through recent years. Depending on their responses, couple decision making was categorized as separate, mutual, or variable (a mixture of separate and mutual). Mutual decisions were those in which both partners participated. Separate decisions were made by individual partners without any sharing between partners. The variable category included a mixture of both mutual and shared decisions. As with other dimensions of relationships, we focused on predominant patterns of relational behaviors over time. Many minor decisions, such as day-to-day matters about households, were made by individuals because of circumstances. Otherwise decisions by these partners tended to be made jointly, especially decisions about significant matters, which are discussed in this chapter.

There was stability in couple decision-making styles over time, which was different from the patterns of communication (see Fig. 4.1). Despite the difficulties gay partners experienced with communication, they were able to come together when significant decisions needed to be made. A high level of mutuality characterized the decision making of more than eight out of ten couples.

Despite the similarities between gays and lesbians in how they made decisions, there was a difference in the processing of decision-making experiences: for lesbians, reflecting upon and learning from their interpersonal experiences, including decision making, was central to the viability of their relationships; gay partners did not reflect as much with each other on how they made decisions.

A lesbian respondent expressed the significance of processing experiences by asking if we had heard the joke: "How many lesbians does it take to change a light bulb? Five . . . one to change the bulb and four to process the experience." She went on to say that she and her partner "process decisions a lot. If anything, we're fairly slow to make decisions, but I think we're very thoughtful. We do a lot of sharing. It's rare when a decision is made only by one of us that would affect both of us." She saw each of them as resourceful information gatherers who proceeded systematically with couple decision making. Mutuality in making important decisions had become increasingly valued, especially during the last several years of their relationship. They also reflected extensively on their strategies of arriving at consensus which were different from those of gay partners. Gays seemed to attend to the decisions themselves and not so much to the method of arriving at decisions. This variance in how gays and lesbians processed their decisions contributed to the differences in the quality of communication between them.

NEGOTIATING ROLES

The interplay of individual decision-making styles and those that evolved between partners was an important dynamic in these relationships. Jennifer and Joyce spoke about the effect of their individual styles on the relationship. If individual differences in styles were not to have a corroding effect on the relationship, they needed to be discussed. Jennifer spoke of how she and Joyce negotiated relational roles while developing an acceptance of individual differences:

> The struggle was my spontaneity, which sometimes was impulsive, so it gave her a pain in the ass. . . . I mean I had to learn a lot. If you can change something, I don't mean give up the good parts of yourself, sort of grow both as an individual and as a couple, to make it fit better . . . I may be more aggressive and more urgent and go at it more until it's done. Joyce sort of circles around and sums it up. I make more mistakes. I think she thinks better and uses a longer approach but gets it done. I go five different shots at it, and then I get it done. I've always been more impulsive and more quick. I think you're wrong more when you do that than somebody who sits back and sizes it up and takes everything into consideration. Over the years we've learned who is good at what . . . we look at everything. Then we just kind of make up our minds. Over the years your antenna gets similar or something. That's the way we've done pretty much everything. Kind of together.

Individual differences led to relational struggles, as Jennifer pointed out, but also contributed positively to a sense of wholeness. Each partner complemented the other: Jennifer helped Joyce to become expressive, and Joyce helped Jennifer to become systematic in making decisions. Often, crises were a catalyst for bringing the significance of differences into consciousness. When Joyce became seriously ill, Jennifer thought of how similar she was to her mother and how much she depended on Joyce as an anchor in their relationship: "it woke up everything in me about how self-absorbed my mother was; it's hard when your partner gets sick." Importantly, reflections on roles and relationships led to negotiating shifts in specific aspects of role behavior and not to sweeping changes in decision-making styles. The processing of differences led, as well, to an acceptance of differences, which was important for adaptation in relationships. Joyce talked about their roles and how they negotiated differences:

> I have a tendency to run decisions into the ground. She can be very direct. Lay it on the table and see what has to get done. When I get in control of my anxiety and push it away, I can do the same thing. But the first thing that kicks in, the legacy of my childhood, the anxiety kicks in. It's harder for me when I see a problem, I tend to see the glass half empty and she'll tend to see the glass is half full . . . it's always been that way, but I've gotten much better at being less anxious . . . we attempt to do things, go along with one another. If someone made up an idea, I might say: "Yeah, that's fine, let's go ahead and do it." She will do the same thing. That's how we've evolved. . . . I tend to hold back and kind of case the joint, so to speak. You know I take my time about it, and Jennifer tends to plunge in. That she carries over, I believe, from her childhood and the way her mother was and all that.

Negotiations between Jennifer and Joyce centered on their individual differences, which had a significant impact on the quality of their roles. Their polarized styles evolved, and in recent years each partner made shifts in individual styles of communicating about decisions. They became aware of their interdependence and how individual differences contributed to their relationship. Both partners modified specific behaviors as they made decisions together without changing important parts of themselves. Developing and maintaining effective communication strengthened their relational connection, a central part of which was acceptance of individual personality differences.

The inability to negotiate individual differences in role behaviors led to a sense of separateness within relationships. Regina talked about that:

> I am real decisive. I am real clear about making decisions, and I am pretty aware of what I want. I think that creates a tension in the relationship. Part of our initial attraction was that I am real analytical and real direct. I don't mean to come across as inflexible, but I think Roberta likes people who are sort of

> organized. Roberta is much more fluid. She is sort of go with the flow type person. I'm kind of: "let's go do this," and I'll kind of do it. Roberta gets intimidated and swept up in the decision-making process. We had a tendency, and I don't think it is a strength, to divide things up. This is your stuff, and this is my stuff . . . it feels real parallel; it doesn't feel real integrated. Like, I will be in charge of this, and you will be in charge of that . . . so decisions get made something like that. Sometimes we just defer to the other . . . we do a lot of parallel stuff: "You do this, and I will do that."

Clearly, Regina was the dominant partner when decisions had to be made. The polarities in their personalities remained, more or less, constant over the seventeen years they have been together. The complementary relationship apparently met their different needs: Regina needed to have power and control; Roberta needed to rely on someone to take care of her and to make decisions. Unlike Jennifer and Joyce and most other couples, Regina and Roberta were not able to negotiate modifications in their behaviors, and, as a consequence, their roles retained a parallel character over the years. Their complementary traits, which had originally attracted them to each other, fed the separateness in their relationship.

Roberta had a similar view of their roles in the relationship:

> I don't make a lot of decisions. I don't have this decision-making process that is very rational. I tend to mull over a problem: "Should I do this, should I do that, what am I going to do with my life?" I tend to ask a lot of people: "What do you think I should do with my life?" . . . and look for some kind of outside stuff. Then it sort of surfaces out of the murk. Regina is logical and systematic about stuff; she is able to take even deeply personal issues and lift them out to a level that is not emotional and make a rational decision about it. She is pretty systematic; she is pretty rational. It's hard to make decisions together . . . that is part of the stuff that has been shoved off into the corners all these years. A lot of them, she just makes the decision and I just say: "OK!" It is easier to go along than it is to try to get in the way of this powerful decision-making engine that she is. In a lot of ways, I have just sort of allowed her decisions to rule, to stand because it is hard for me to figure out what I want, or for me to be very direct about what I want. There have been big pieces of our lives where we say: "OK, you are in charge for the day . . . you are the queen and I

am the helper . . . the next project, I will be the queen and you
be the helper."

Roberta experienced difficulty in being direct with Regina about what
she wanted out of the relationship. Swept up by what she perceived as
the dynamism of her partner, Roberta deferred to Regina, yet resented
her. Perhaps her need to be taken care of and fear of losing someone
who met those needs prevented Roberta from being assertive in the
relationship. As she observed, they avoided confronting the delicate
balance by not addressing these issues and by maintaining separateness
in their roles, especially those that involved making decisions. Their
connection was grounded on maintaining parallel roles that included
taking turns with various tasks and responsibilities. In contrast to
Jennifer and Joyce who came together in spite of differences, Regina
and Roberta were unable to negotiate shifts in their role behaviors
toward a middle ground and apparently found security in maintaining
separate territories.

Modifications in decision-making roles were frequently reported as
individuals talked about their relationships from their early years together through recent years. Frank and Fred, together for nineteen
years, described how modifications had been negotiated in their roles.
Frank said:

> The first five years I think I made most of the decisions and Fred
> followed. He always had plenty to say. . . . I mean, he had plenty
> of input into making the decisions, but the actual decision, the
> final word, is what I did. We were together a couple of years
> when Fred started putting his input in . . . at the beginning, I didn't
> like it, because he was putting his nose in my business . . . now,
> most of the petty decision, the operating decisions, Fred takes
> care of that kind of thing. It's changed from time to time. It used
> to be I would get all that kind of thing, and now Fred is doing
> that. We share more and, it isn't as important anymore who does
> what projects.

Themes of territory and power were important dynamics in negotiating
roles between these partners. During the early years, Frank, who was
perceived as the more powerful partner, made most of the decisions,
although Fred participated in the process leading up to the actual
decisions. The potential was probably always present in the relationship
for Frank to give up power and for Fred to become more assertive. Had

the rigidity in their complementary and imbalanced roles persisted, as it did between Regina and Roberta, this couple may also have developed a separate and parallel relational structure. The shift toward mutuality in their relationship began several years before the retirement of the older partner, Frank, who originally had been the dominant one. Certainly his retirement and decision to be at home reinforced that modification.

Fred's observations about the shift toward greater mutuality in their roles mirrored those of his partner:

> Communicating about decisions has changed. We think about it longer; we weigh the pros and cons a little longer, rather than just jumping in head first. There are still those decisions that we do just jump right in, head first, but they're smaller, inconsequential decisions rather than big decisions. We've become more mature. . . . Frank had a lot of influence over everything at the beginning of the relationship. As time has progressed, there are areas now that I have total influence, like the finances. . . . I grew up in a household that was very catch as catch can. To me it wasn't a big deal whether the fork went on the left side of the plate or the right, as long as it was on the table. Frank was raised in a different environment. He has taught me, and I don't mean negatively . . . it's sort of evened out.

As Fred mentioned, maturity had a lot to do with changes that occurred in their relationship. There was a "mellowing" of the personalities of these men as they grew older. They became more thoughtful and reflective about decisions; Frank had less need to control his partner, and Fred developed greater confidence in making decisions. Change was possible because both partners were "willing" to modify specific behaviors. Fred also pointed out that they came from very different family backgrounds, which had significant effects on which partner became dominant in the relationship. In middle age, each partner developed skills in communicating more effectively with the other, being sensitive to each other's needs, and negotiating a new balance in roles and responsibilities.

Exploring how roles shifted as well as how they remained the same was an important part of understanding how relationships evolved over time. Needs for autonomy along with equally strong needs for connection in a meaningful relationship were important dynamics in the modification of roles. Gwen and Grace identified the interplay of these two powerful forces in their relationship from early to recent years:

> Grace took the lead in more things in the beginning all the way around. I was happy to be there, and I was, not exactly a follower, but I followed at that point. In the middle years we got into a lot of: "I want to do it this way; no, I want to do it this way." The attachment couldn't exactly go forward. . . . I think we probably separated out roles. I let her take the lead in some ways, and I took the lead in other ways. This is a little oversimplified, but probably in the recent years . . . it happened at thirteen or fourteen years . . . that we are much more able to actually and more totally do things together, taking both people into consideration. . . . Grace likes to process things together more than I like to. I would just as soon work it out, like, here's how it is. She wants to do it together. We have learned how to come to the middle a little more, or else we will do it my way this time or your way the next time. Those are the three options you have, or we will keep fighting each other.

In discussing her observations, Gwen identified a critical dynamic in the relationships of many couples. Generally, partners felt they had found someone whom they did not want to lose. Even individuals who valued their autonomy, such as Gwen, decided to temper their natural style of relating in order to preserve the relationship. If they "allowed" their assertiveness to emerge, many partners feared the other partner might be driven away. In order to avoid that threat, they submerged an important part of themselves, only to have it reemerge during the middle years. Then negotiating role modifications was based on respecting differences and allowing each partner space to express their individuality within relationships. It was not unusual for those modifications in roles to take years as individuals gradually felt safe and confident enough to allow their true selves to emerge. Even then, respondents did not feel they needed to change fundamental elements in their personalities; rather, they modified individual behaviors and reactions to one another in order to make mutual decisions.

Experiences and roles in past relationships had a significant effect on most relationships. The process of negotiating new and satisfying balances in role relations was discussed by Grace:

> Both of us are strong and intuitive about what is right for us. If we can figure out all the options and all the choices, what feels right

for us, we can go forward. But if we can't find a way for it to feel right, we can't just get settled. We never understood that we are very different about the things that matter sometimes. Priorities seem really different. We are both good problem solvers in that we believe things can be solved, and we are very creative with options. . . . Our actual methods of how we start are usually very different . . . like, doing the mortgage: Gwen would get facts and figures, and I, half the time, would only remember the global aspect of things. For me that is not important. . . . I would know more in my gut level. Even if it cost more, this is gonna be right for me. I couldn't ever articulate it. She would be saying: "Why are we going to pay double. There is no logic to this." It would be very frustrating. Probably because I never had to verbalize it so much before. I never had to accommodate to somebody in a way that was so different. I hadn't gotten that close to anybody. . . . With my ex-husband and I, there wasn't much discussion. He just did his things and I did mine, and we didn't really try to merge things. We didn't really try to make couple decisions. We had separate ways of doing things. So I think it was the first time I had to articulate my way to somebody that was so different. I think she felt the same way. I think it was hard for her to be with somebody for whom facts and figures were not really relevant. . . . The second five years, I felt that I wasted a little bit of my time trying to make things work. I should have seen the handwriting on the wall. Why try to get some mutual agreement about something where I could have just said: "It is mine; I'll do it my way." Or: "It is yours; you do it your way." We found that to be much more satisfying, and it works much better. I was just so unwilling to do that then. I was just unwilling to . . . give up on trying to convince her that it is going to be good for us.

Change between Gwen and Grace evolved slowly throughout the years as each partner learned how to express her needs. Although they struggled to make decisions jointly, their efforts were compromised by needs to retain individual autonomy and, as importantly, by individual differences. Individual differences and ingrained values about separateness clashed with the need for connectedness within these relationships. Couples used various ways of coping with the tensions between these powerful dynamics, which frequently took years.

For a few couples, modifications from separateness to mutuality in making decisions did not happen, even when they spent time negotiating their roles. For example, Harriet acknowledged that Hillary and she were "not very good at making decisions." She went on to say that

"Hillary tends to come up with the ideas; she tends to have the more innovative ideas. I tend to say no and then, slowly, get convinced; we negotiate a lot." Hillary observed that there was "no hierarchy in our relationship in terms of who the boss is, so it's a struggle . . . to make decisions. It's tough, so we do things by default. . . . We've never learned how to do it well." The rigidity and similarity of their individual styles undermined attempts to negotiate roles toward a middle ground that was described by most couples. As Hillary talked about their relationship, her description of Harriet appeared very similar to Harriet's description of her: "we struggle to make the other one make the decision so that we won't be responsible . . . it's more by default. . . . I tend to see myself as a slow problem solver. Harriet tends to want to jump in and fix things quickly, and sometimes I disagree with the way she is. . . . I think I'm a little more contemplative." Perhaps differences in role behaviors obscured underlying similarities, which prevented this couple from moving toward greater mutuality in their relationship. Similar needs based on characterological traits may have contributed to stability in this and some other relationships. Constant negotiations without modification in role behaviors may have been a form of connection, even though it resulted in much tension between them. Despite their inability to develop mutuality in their relationship, Hillary and Harriet developed enough tolerance about their differences to remain together and be relatively happy.

DECIDING TO HAVE CHILDREN

One out of two lesbian couples in this study had children. The decision to become parents was often complicated and lengthy. Powerful factors shaped that process: bad memories from one's childhood, the effects of child rearing on one's career, and the reactions of other people to a child of a lesbian couple. Regina referred to some of these factors as she talked about becoming a mother:

> It took her a long time to get pregnant . . . it took me years of saying no and finally saying: "Okay, I think that I can handle this, and I know you really want to do that." First, I had to believe that I could handle a kid. I grew up in a crazy household, and I felt so compelled to give a kid what a kid deserves which is love, attention, and security. I really give a lot, and I am really, really present. I have been working part-time pretty much since Melissa was born just because I think it is so important to be there. For

me, to give what a kid needs is a lot of work. . . . You read the literature about kids raised in gay families. It's real interesting stuff. Gay people choose to have kids. Its not like somebody got pregnant on Saturday night. We thought it through and we chose to raise Melissa; it is something we are really committed to. I think that we can give her some opportunities. Its amazing what happens to kids when you are nice to them.

The significance of decisions to have a child was different from that of other decisions couples made. As discussed earlier in this chapter, Regina and Roberta had a way of making decisions that included a high level of separateness. Regina assumed a dominant role in making decisions, and Roberta tended to go along with her wishes. Over the years they resolved their differences through negotiating a compromise, so that Roberta was empowered to assume a dominant role in the relationship from time to time. Through the process of deciding to become a mother, Regina needed to make peace with the apprehensions from her childhood experiences in a family that, she felt, did not offer her enough love. She needed to weigh the strong desire of Roberta to become a mother and her own reluctance to become a parent. These two factors needed considerable time to be resolved. Negotiating to become parents went forward within the context of a relationship that included ongoing differences in the roles of partners.

Roberta commented on the lengthy process of deciding to become parents:

The first issue was that Regina didn't like kids. . . . She saw no reason to have people under thirty in your life . . . we talked that one back and forth maybe for ten years: "I really want to have a kid; I don't; let's buy a house first; okay, I still want to have a kid; I don't; maybe I could have a kid, but you wouldn't have to be his parent; yeah, right, but the toys would still be in the house; maybe we would have separate houses, and you could have the kid at your house." At some point I said: "I cannot make this decision to have a kid." Regina said: "Clearly, we are not going to stay together unless you do have a kid . . . you are going to have one. OK, we'll do it." That was long and just a series of conversations over years and years and years.

Although the issues of having a child were similar to those of other couples, parenthood for this couple, Roberta and Regina, had a significance quite different from that of most couples who became parents, particularly in relation to power and control themes. The relationship may have ended if Roberta did not have a child. Despite her dominance in other matters, Regina agreed to her partner becoming a mother through in vitro fertilization after acknowledging Roberta's need for a child and the importance of a child to their relationship.

Other couples shared a mutual goal from the early years of their relationship to become mothers. Samantha said, "we both could never imagine ourselves as not being mothers; that's something we talked about from the beginning of our relationship," which was eighteen years ago. She went on to talk about how they would reach their goal: "We had the problem of who was going to go first. We both really wanted that. That seems unusual with lesbian couples; most have one person who wants to do the child bearing, and the other person is fine with that." Both partners had strong desires for motherhood, so the task was to decide who was to get pregnant. In contrast to Regina and Roberta, there was little, if any, ambivalence in becoming parents. Therapy helped them to resolve the issue of who would get pregnant first.

Sarah described the steps along the way to becoming parents:

> The first thing was deciding if we could have children in the context of a lesbian relationship. That was the first step. Then, could we have children? When we could, how were we going to do it? We were both sure we wanted to have children. There was not the trouble some people have of are we going to do it. We were very sure but not sure how we were going to pull it off and be in a relationship together. But I guess we were committed to doing it together.
>
> Then there was the issue of who was going to get pregnant first, which was really, really hard. For me it was kind of prioritizing what I really wanted because we assumed, correctly, that Samantha was going to get pregnant quickly, and it would take me a long time. That was what ultimately happened. I decided I just wanted to have a baby, and I wanted to get it done. . . . The other decisions were more simple because it wasn't like you had to give anything up to make them.

The contrast in decision making with that of heterosexual couples was vivid in the comments of Sarah about parenthood. The process of having a child in the context of a lesbian relationship was of great significance, not so much because of the sexual orientation of couples but because of the lack of societal support and the ever-present danger of prejudice, especially toward their children. Becoming a parent, regardless of the method used, involved significant sacrifices and challenges for these women.

The sacrifices and challenges of parenthood for lesbian couples were portrayed in the responses of Octavia and Olivia to our questions about parenthood. Octavia talked about several issues lesbian couples had to consider when they thought of having a child:

> It was really something I wanted to do. There are a ton of decisions . . . there is no right answer, and each option has its drawbacks . . . we spent about two years going down all the paths. Were we going to adopt, which we were seriously going to consider but then the state said that homosexuals may not adopt. It was horrible, and there we were thinking about having kids in a state where these two wonderful men who had taken in these foster kids . . . a wonderful, loving family . . . were found out to be gay; the kids were yanked out of the home. We were torn when that happened. So that closed the adoption door to us. We said that we were not going to do anything where our kids could be taken away from us. Then, which one of us could be pregnant. It was easier for me being pregnant. It was like I want the kid, I'll go through it. I didn't know what I was talking about. Then we had to decide about a known or unknown donor, and that was really hard. We had a lot of decisions to make that were very heavy. Even with an unknown donor, there was the possibility of getting a Yes Donor which means at the age of eighteen, the child, if he wants to, could find out the identity of the father. It was sort of hard in trying to think what was the best decision for us.

Lesbian couples had to contend with several issues in becoming parents. Looming in the background of these decisions were the clouds of homophobia and societal attitudes toward same-sex couples becoming parents. With the publicity surrounding the removal of foster children from the home of a gay couple, Octavia and Olivia were confronted with the potential consequences of adoption. The decision to become parents through in vitro fertilization of Octavia confronted them with a range of additional issues. As she said: "there were no easy options, and each one had its drawbacks."

Olivia spoke of similar issues as Octavia along with additional ones:

> When we started exploring this idea of having kids, some things had to change. We had to move from where we lived. . . . There were lots of decisions to make around who was going to have the kid: were we going to have a biological child? we decided yes; who was going to have it? if we were going to use a known donor or an unknown donor? and on and on. We went through those steps . . . and we talked to a lot of people who had kids . . . it was a really good thing to do. . . . Making decisions like that can be difficult . . . especially around the known donor versus the unknown donor. I remember sitting down together making lists of pros and cons. . . . I don't think it was a situation where Octavia was trying to convince me or I was trying to convince her. . . . It was more like: what about this; what about that. The only issue, I think, that was hard was the last name. We ended up hyphenating the name . . . she didn't want to do that, and I did . . . that was laborious in terms of having to make decisions.

Deciding to become parents confronted lesbian couples with many challenges. All of them had to contend with social realities not supportive of the rights of homosexuals to become parents and to rear children. Within that negative atmosphere, lesbian partners had to contend with issues similar to those that face all prospective parents. Lesbians needed to decide about parenthood within the context of their relationships: whether to adopt or choose another method; who was to become pregnant if they chose in vitro fertilization; the potential consequences of a known or unknown donor; how to reallocate relational roles to make room for parenting. A major issue, identified by Olivia, was in deciding on the last name of their child. The name was a manifestation of the connection between parent and child. It had powerful meaning to both the biological mother and her partner. The resolution for this couple was to use both of their names, which represented their mutual investment in and contribution to their child. Skills in communicating, commitment to relationships, willingness to engage in decision making often over a long period of time, mutual concern for the well-being of each partner, and a systematic approach to resolving issues associated with parenthood were important resources in making these decisions.

FINANCES

Given the high levels of education and professional employment of most respondents, the economic well-being of couples was not a surprise. Poverty as an oppressive force was practically nonexistent among them. Annually, 50 percent of the combined incomes of both partners was more than $75,000. No couple had an income below $25,000. There was a weak association between income levels of couples and the effect of money on relationships. More lower-income partners reported negative effects of money on relationships than did higher-income partners; more higher-income couples, those over $75,000, reported a positive influence of money on relationships.

An important aspect of decision making was related to the meaning of money within the context of relationships as a whole. Although joint income of couples had little effect on the quality of relationships, differences, as well as similarities, in individual incomes affected decision making about spending money and reflected important relational themes between partners. These themes included power, autonomy, mutuality, and equity, which were evident as respondents spoke about the meaning of money to their relationships.

Individuals with higher incomes appeared generally to have more power in relationships than did their lower-income partners. The association between money and power was identified by Deirdre:

> I didn't have as much money as she did. To me, that gave her power. . . . For a while, there was an inequality of income, such that I was going in debt trying to keep up with her . . . making sure I paid for at least half of everything . . . it got a little contentious, and we got into: "Well, I can't go; I'm sorry I don't have enough money." She would say: "I'll pay for it." I hated that. Somewhere along the line she finally had a switch around in attitude toward yours, mine, and ours . . . the lines became more and more blurred, and so it is no longer a problem.

Income differences tended to magnify inequities and had the potential to undermine mutuality. Unless the psychological significance of income differences was discussed, it had a potentially corrosive effect on the development of mutuality in relationships. An important dynamic of mutuality was in the "blurring" of boundaries between partners in aspects of relationships; that "blurring" was a threat to personal autonomy within relationships, a theme that emerged in several interviews, mostly with lesbians. Preserving autonomy was important, although its form varied depending on individual needs.

Regina talked of having separate bank accounts as a way of maintaining autonomy:

> We both have separate checking accounts; then each month each of us writes a check to a joint account to which bills get paid . . . I think it is sort of an autonomy issue. I want to make sure I can spend my money anyway I want, so I don't have to give up the autonomy. You sort of give up so much other stuff in the relationship. I want to know that, if I want to buy something, that I can go and write a check, and no one is going to say anything about what I buy. Straight couples mix their money so much, but I don't know if I would want it. Maybe it creates a more shared sense of we are all in this together. A big piece of what happens with us is that we keep so much autonomy that there is not so much "we are all in it together" feeling.

Preserving autonomy appeared as important to Regina as the development of mutuality, a theme evident in the relationships of most lesbians. For this couple as well as others, there was a dynamic balance between autonomy and mutuality that needed to be negotiated as relationships evolved. Partners developed mutuality when they experienced themselves as coming together on matters central to their relationships. The development of mutuality was nurtured as the significance of money to relationships was discussed and negotiated. Important to a sense of mutuality between partners, especially for those with lower incomes, was to contribute equitably to relationships. The twin dynamics of mutuality and equity were prominent themes as respondents talked about incomes and decisions to spend money. Kate and Kristin spoke about these themes. Kate said:

> I may have had more influence where money is concerned, because I've had a little more at my disposal . . . it was hard a few years ago when I wanted to do some work on the house, and she couldn't do her fair share. We'd always done it together. We were able to talk it through though, and she was able to let me do it, even though she couldn't contribute her share. That was very hard for her to do that. . . . Once Kristin was able to say: "OK, we'll do this; you can spend your money if you want to . . . but I don't have it to spend." We've never had any concerns.

The threat of differences in incomes to the strong value of mutuality between partners was evident in what Kate said. In fact, her higher income was as much an issue for her as fairness was to Kristin. Income differences triggered discussions of these issues between partners. Among lesbians, in particular, it was very important to discuss those differences in order to feel that decisions about expenditures were made fairly. Kristin spoke of the importance of equity in sharing expenses:

> It's very important to me to pay my share, and to pay my way.
> . . . My first response to doing stuff in the house was, no, I'd rather if we had extra money to travel. It finally dawned on me that wasn't really fair, because she had the money; she wanted to do it; this was going to please her. Whether it was important to me or not, I was finally able to say: "OK, that's what you want to do." We both have had comparable incomes . . . if I don't think I'm paying my share, that gets me upset, which doesn't have that much to do with the money, but rather am I carrying my weight ? . . . At the beginning of the relationship we used to keep a record of who paid for what . . . after a couple of years, we said: "Why on earth are we wasting this time and energy?" We don't do that anymore.

For Kristin and many lesbian partners, paying one's fair share symbolized dynamics of power, autonomy, mutuality, and equity. There was a subtle difference in the significance of these themes between gays and lesbians. Lesbians spoke often about the process of negotiating differences in order to preserve and enhance mutuality in their relationships. In contrast, gays said they had handled money mutually from the early years to the present. The issue of integrating autonomy with mutuality was not identified as much between gay partners as it was between lesbians. Barry described how he and Brian dealt with finances:

> I don't believe we've ever had a financial problem . . . we've both had periods of unemployment, but we've always been able to pay our rent; we've always had plenty to eat; we agree on our charities that we give to. Financially, we've never had any problem at all. Everything is jointly held. He's the sole beneficiary of my will. I'm the sole beneficiary of his will. All moneys are held together. All stocks and bonds, all jointly held.

Most lesbians did not talk this way about managing money. For them, issues of money were part of the process of resolving themes related to power, autonomy, mutuality, and fairness. As the relationships of lesbian partners developed over the years, joint bank accounts resulted from the development of mutuality. Most gays decided to manage their finances jointly from the beginning of their relationships. Brian mirrored what Barry had said about managing finances:

No real problem. We have a very simple life. We do not spend a lot of money. We have simple wants, simple tastes. We do not have major debts other than the monthly stuff like everybody else . . . we know what we always have in front of us and when you have to just pull back a little . . . part of the reason for that is because it is one sum of money. It is not his money, my money, it is our money, and we always emphasize that. That works for us.

The differences between gays and lesbians on the issue of handling money may have been related to the significance of preserving autonomy for women compared to men. For women, independence and autonomy within relationships were highly valued. While those values may apply to women in general, they were certainly central in the lives of the women in this study. Highly educated individuals who held responsible positions in their professions, they were acknowledged and rewarded for their competence. Accomplishments in their careers reinforced contemporary values about power, autonomy, and fairness that characterize modern women in this society. Their challenge was to integrate those qualities with the equally powerful value of mutuality in these relationships.

Because of discrimination toward women, lesbians may have felt more vulnerable than gays unless there was an equitable distribution of power based on different resources that each partner contributed to relationships. Thus it was understandable that so many lesbians commented on the importance of equity in assessing what each partner brought to and took from relationships. For lesbians, money was symbolic of relational issues that were worked out over the years. The differing ways in which gays talked about financial decisions probably reflected traditional societal values about power, autonomy, and fairness in relationships. Men did not think of power in relationships in the same way as women. Gays may have assumed an equitable distribution of these qualities within their relationships; lesbians had to work at integrating these qualities into relationships in which mutuality was equally valued. It is also possible that the mutual handling of money by gays was a way of trying to avoid the conflict that was inevitable as partners dealt with differences over the years.

SUMMARY

Differences were apparent in the patterns of communication between gay and lesbian partners from early to recent years, although their decision-making styles were quite similar. During the early years, about half of all respondents reported significant difficulties in communicating with their partners. As relationships unfolded, the quality of communication between partners was regarded more positively by lesbians than it was by gays. During the middle years, considerable regression was reported by gay partners, while the quality of communication between lesbians remained as it was during the early years. In recent years, the quality of communication between gays returned to the levels reported when partners were first together; at that time, communication improved dramatically between lesbians. These communication patterns probably reflected the differences between males and females in relational skills, which have been associated with gender: women seem to be more skilled at interpersonal communication compared to men. The regression in the middle years reported by gays was related to conflicts in relationships, including sexual affairs, about which gays had difficulty communicating. Lesbians seemed to have more investment in and skill at working out conflicts.

Making decisions mutually as a couple required effective communication skills in relatively specific aspects of relationships, such as negotiating roles and handling finances. For half the lesbians in this study, decisions about becoming parents were also a reality. The patterns of mutuality in making decisions were similar for gays and lesbians, but the involvement of each partner in the process varied between the two groups. The variability was not in the decision making itself but in the process of reflecting upon and learning from experiences of making decisions as a couple. In negotiating roles, partners needed to become involved in discussing their individual differences in order to make decisions about changing specific behaviors. Learning to accept innate differences that would not change was as important as modifying specific behaviors. One change was in learning to respect and accept a partner through open and honest discussion of differences.

For women who were mothers, decision making about parenthood was central in their relationships for considerable periods of time. Unlike other matters that needed to be decided between partners, motherhood was complicated by social policies, laws, and attitudes about same-sex parents. Decisions always had to be made within the context of laws and court rulings that were hostile toward and threatening to lesbian parents. The investment in processing experiences and skill at communication were valuable resources in helping lesbian couples make decisions about parenthood.

Finally, the study uncovered several dynamic issues in these relationships related to managing finances. Gays appeared to make decisions about money that focused on balancing contributions of partners to relationships. When incomes were very uneven, gay partners tended to look to other forms of contributions that promoted equity in relationships. Gay decision making did not seem as complicated as that of lesbian couples. As lesbians discussed the significance of incomes and decision making about spending money, the themes of power, autonomy, mutuality, and equity emerged. Perhaps the explicit connections that several lesbian respondents made between these four dynamics reflected the orientation of women to process their relational experiences in general. Lesbians were oriented to understanding the meaning behind those aspects of their relationships; gays, on the other hand, tended to be empirical in making decisions about finances. For them, a dollar was a dollar, but for lesbians a dollar represented something about their life together that needed to be understood. Given their values about the importance of mutuality in their relationships, lesbians spent more time than did gays in negotiating decisions related to the meaning of the unevenness of incomes to power, autonomy, and fairness. Even among lesbian partners who had relatively equal incomes, these dynamics shaped how finances were managed.

5

Conflict

If something pissed me off, I said it. And she had trouble with that.

In these relationships, as in any relationship that lasts, conflict emerged from differences between partners. Given the high levels of complementarity in role behaviors, conflict was inevitable. States of interpersonal disharmony were manifested in several forms as relationships evolved during the early, middle, and recent years.

Our challenge was to assess the severity of conflict. A distinction was made between minimal and major conflict on the basis of how partners perceived the severity of problems, tensions, and differences between them. If respondents described conflict as highly distressing and having significant disruptive effects on their relationships, the conflict was considered major. If differences did not have these effects on a respondent and the relationship, the conflicts were considered minor.

An example of major conflict was taken from an interview in which Esther described how different her partner and she were. Their relationship has lasted sixteen years. Differences were contained at tolerable levels throughout their early years together. During the middle years, one partner became obsessed with another woman and described the major disruption that occurred:

I got obsessed with someone. I guess you could say attracted, not sexually attracted, but absolutely obsessed with wanting to know this person's life. I really got caught up in it. A large percentage of my mental energy went to this for a couple of years. A lot of attention was diverted from our relationship. . . . So Elly was feeling starved. I wasn't really dealing with our relationship and how to make it better and wasn't sure what we had in common. Elly was ticked at me most of the time either veiled or unveiled. There were always these periods when she would get furious and emotional. My first reaction was to shut down, and then she kind of kept it up until I broke down. She was probably increasingly distrustful; she was really thrown into a tailspin when I told her about this woman that I was obsessed with. That was a major, major violation in her mind. Of course, I had been honorable in this, but that very much undermined the sense of trust because she felt I had been deceitful, which I was, by not telling her. So at that time she said: "Well, if this happens again, you should tell me." Then one day I saw this woman again and was again very attracted, so I dutifully reported this, and she went into another tailspin.

As with other aspects of these relationships, our intent was to understand conflict from the perspectives of individual partners, that is, from the inside out rather than from the outside in.

In this chapter, we begin by reviewing the patterns of major conflict from early to recent years. The perceptions of respondents about the potential effects of homophobia on them and their relationships are presented, followed by the types of relational conflict they experienced. These conflicts included differences about money, sexuality including monogamy, child rearing, and the effects of personal problems on relationships. After discussing the types of conflict, we explore how partners managed conflict with a focus on the dynamics that contributed to avoidant behaviors common in these relationships during the early and middle years. Finally, we examine the means through which avoidant behaviors were modified in recent years.

CONFLICT OVER TIME

Figure 5.1 shows the pattern of major conflict from early to recent years. Major conflict increased among both gays and lesbians during the middle years of their relationships. Fifty-eight percent of lesbians and 46 percent of gays reported major conflict during the middle years.

Figure 5.1
Major Conflict between Partners

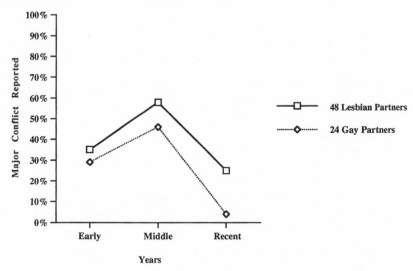

In recent years, one out of four lesbian partners continued to experience major conflict; only one gay partner described major conflict during those years.

The increase in major conflict during the middle years had a negative effect on several aspects of these relationships. Conflict was associated with a decline in physical and psychological intimacy. Perceptions of relational values in a partner and in oneself also suffered. Respondents who reported major conflict did not see their partners or themselves as trustful, respectful, understanding, or as sensitive as those who did not report major conflict; nor were they as satisfied as other respondents. Major conflict and how conflict was handled had a significant impact on relationships and had the potential to undermine the development of relationships in recent years.

A gay couple spoke about the patterns of conflict in their relationship over the years. Each partner felt that communication had been reasonably good between them from the early years. Frank remembered that:

> Our communication has always been pretty good; that was one
> of the things that fit from the onset. Don't ask me why or how, but
> it just sort of went together.

Fred agreed about the quality of communication during the early years:

> We've always kind of fed off each other, and listened . . . we may not like what the other person's saying, but we've listened to each other.

As the relationship evolved beyond the first few years, their individual modes of dealing with personal differences led to major conflict. Although they felt that their communication was "pretty good" from early to recent years, they experienced significant difficulties in contending with their different styles of expressing anger during the middle years. Frank said that:

> We went through a period of time when I felt like I was being abused. . . . It was just a pattern that he got into that was knifing. . . . So we had to talk that one out in counseling, to get through that part of it. That process of going to the counseling service to find out about these things helped us to solve things in the future. We were able to not be aggressive toward each other in discussions; to be able to listen and then, maybe not agree, but to listen.

In referring to the middle years of their relationship, Fred remembered that:

> the second five years was: "Well I don't want to deal with this, so I'll read a magazine." At that time we were going through therapy. He would have a session, and I would have a session, and then we'd have one together. I would just go right over and rip a magazine out of his hands and say: "Now we're going to talk. I'm pissed off! The therapist said that you're not supposed to hide behind a magazine anymore, so I'm takin' it away." Then the last ten years, you just work through all that garbage. I'm not one to sit there and fester about something now. When I'm upset, now, it comes out. . . . I don't want to sit and brood on it for a week. If I'm ticked off, he knows about it immediately.

During recent years, each partner reported changes in their styles of managing conflict. As with many respondents, psychotherapy had a significant impact on patterns of dealing with feelings, especially angry ones, which had become a source of major conflict. In referring to the modification in their styles of managing conflict, Frank commented about the improvement in their communication. Psychotherapy helped partners to become aware of their needs and to learn how to express them constructively. In referring to the relationship at the present time,

Frank said that "communication is a little better now that we know each other better; we have a tendency to speak in shorthand to each other because we know each other so well." Fred viewed modifications in their relationship differently. In talking about recent interactions, he focused initially on his perception of change in Frank, but then went on to acknowledge his difficulties in adapting to the assertiveness of Frank, which had come about as a result of therapy. Fred reported that his partner had "gotten better." "He used to just sit there and internalize it." Fred then acknowledged that it was "still an adjustment for me, when he comes out and confronts me directly. There are times I really like that, but I don't like it when it's directed at me."

Developing effective communication skills was an important part of the process of modifying behavior. It was most successful when individual partners became aware of themselves in the relationship and took responsibility for confronting feelings that were avoided in the past. This process happened between Frank and Fred. Each partner described modifications in their individual behaviors, their awareness of how their behaviors contributed to conflict, and an acknowledgment of what it meant to change.

A lesbian couple who have been together eighteen years spoke of modifications in their relationship from the early years to the present time. Although the content of difficulties between them was different, the underlying themes were similar to those of Frank and Fred. Maria remembered the early years:

> We had a good time together, and there were never any fights, problems, or anything like that . . . we hadn't talked about a lot of things. We just didn't see any reason to talk about them so we didn't. . . . Initially, it was more conversational. We shared a lot of information and told each other things we did and talked about politics, about hiking, about places, about stuff that was going on and about our work, but not very much about feelings.

Maria identified a critical element in the unfolding of conflict to which other respondents also referred. Early years were often remembered as happy ones in which partners were trying to adapt to life together. In the interest of maintaining harmony between them, partners often avoided conflict they feared might threaten the mutual sense of harmony they wished to preserve. For most respondents, these relationships were the most positive and meaningful of their adult lives. Issues that triggered strong feelings that might jeopardize these relationships were avoided. Often years passed before partners were able to confront feelings they assumed were a threat to relational stability. Maria described how the relationship changed, as they struggled to find different ways of dealing with conflict:

> During the second phase, we had to face a lot of difficult feelings in which we weren't very graceful talking about and didn't talk about anymore than we needed to. But we did start talking more about what was going on . . . our relationship and intimacy were some of the things we hadn't talked about. She was doing that out of the desperate grasp of doing something for me because she cared for me. . . . So when we started to face that emotional stuff, we didn't have a history or experience in that and weren't very good at talking about those things even in the best of times. We had never practiced, and things began to spiral more and more out of control and was aggravated by the fact that Molly was in a job that she hated, and so was I . . . we had excuses of why there wasn't time to talk.

Maria identified how difficult it was to initiate discussion about unpleasant feelings, such as anger toward a partner, that might threaten the stability of the relationship. Respondents commented frequently on how unprepared they were emotionally to face conflict. In contrast to intellectual discussions, the emotional language used in confronting unpleasant aspects of relationships was neither graceful nor easy. The fear of losing control, and ultimately of losing the relationship, loomed in the background. As Maria and Molly struggled to discuss aspects of their relationship during the middle years that they feared threatened its stability, they decided to have a child:

> The communication sort of changed when we decided to have a child . . . it was not something that you can just fall into. . . . So one of the things that is good about this is it makes you talk about it. It was good for us. We had to talk about it and then actually go ahead and plan it and decided to do it . . . all the myriad of decisions that needed to be made . . . all the things that we had not explicitly talked about for ourselves. So that has been good. I think it has spilled over into more explicitly talking about what each of us wants.

For this couple, the joint decision to have a child provided an opportunity to bring them together on relational matters in addition to parenthood. To have experienced success in communicating about becoming parents had a positive effect on their confidence to deal with other less pleasant aspects of their relationship. As Maria said, the reality of deciding to become parents was a catalyst for facing matters they previously avoided discussing.

Molly reflected on the quality of their relationship in recent years:

> Now emotional intimacy is probably there, too. It has probably been there throughout. It's not probably as open as some relationships, but we certainly rely on each other enormously for our emotional well-being. I certainly rely on Maria to help me out when I am feeling crummy or whatever. The sexual intimacy has certainly gone up and down. A lot of it depends on how well we are getting along. Certainly there was more of it early on in the relationship . . . and then there was not very much sex in our relationship for several years . . . now its regaining itself. We are getting along very well these days.

The observations of the partners in these two relationships illustrated the changes that took place over the years. Major conflict increased significantly during the middle years and then declined in recent years. Of importance were the differences between gays and lesbians in how conflict was described. Across the years, more lesbians described major conflict than did gays. Although that difference may reflect the reality of higher levels of major conflict between lesbian partners compared to gays, we think it reflected how men and women perceived, evaluated, and discussed conflict. Lesbians more than gays may have acknowledged the presence of serious difficulties in relationships even when other aspects of relationships were not conflictual. Gays, on the other hand, talked about the resolution of conflict in more sweeping ways. Compared to gays, lesbians tolerated a broader range of human emotions and accepted imperfection in relationships, even in recent years after many positive behavioral modifications. For example, Molly acknowledged difficulties with interpersonal openness and intimacy along with positive changes in their relationship. Women not only had more tolerance for relational imperfections but less need to deny the presence of conflict within relationships.

HOMOPHOBIA

We explored how prevailing social norms and attitudes about same-sex relationships contributed to relational conflict. Society did not and does not recognize the legitimacy of committed relationships between gay and lesbian partners. As a consequence, gay and lesbian couples were not legally entitled to benefits heterosexual couples took for granted. For example, mortgages, insurance, pensions, and other survivor benefits that heterosexual spouses have been entitled to through marriage were treated as separate property in same-sex relationships, unless partners initiated action to modify their policies. In addition to differences based on social policies, gays and lesbians suffered from prejudice and discrimination because they were different from the dominant social group. Fears that fueled hostile attitudes toward them as a minority group originated from numerous sources. A fundamental source was sexual orientation, which was as critical and powerful to homosexuals as it was to heterosexuals. For the dominant heterosexual group, difference in this fundamental element of identity was treated with contempt and rejection.

A consequence of being different in a way that challenged heterosexual identity was homophobia. The fear of homosexuality was manifested in the form of social attitudes and behaviors that discriminated against gays and lesbians. When respondents were struggling with their sexual orientations, they were exposed inevitably to homophobic attitudes. Frequently they internalized these attitudes, which created psychological turmoil about a fundamental element in their makeup as men and women who also happened to be gays and lesbians. As a consequence, these individuals had to contend with negative and ambivalent feelings within themselves about their sexual orientations.

Social and psychological homophobia created stress for gay and lesbian relationships. Although homophobia, in itself, was not reported as a major conflict, homophobic attitudes and behaviors created a social and interpersonal context that was generally stressful to gay and lesbian partners. In their efforts to work out interpersonal difficulties, partners did not feel their relationships were supported or validated by society. A number of individuals struggled with internalized homophobia, which needed to be addressed before other problems could be resolved.

Deirdre talked of the personal effects of social homophobia in her relationship with Daphne. As is true for most, if not all people, the identity and self-respect of Deirdre were intimately connected to her work and career. The threat of being "identified" as a homosexual was constant. There were differences in how open each partner was about their sexual orientation. Remaining closeted caused stress, as Deirdre described:

Both of us have always been aware that, as we have climbed in our careers, there was always a chance of somebody coming and knocking our pins right out from under us by revealing our homosexuality. That has always been there, that is always hanging over you. As a matter of fact, when I got promoted, I had a visit almost immediately from a young man who didn't get the position who thought he had it in his pocket. He threatened to go to the executive committee at that moment and oust me. . . . It adds a tremendous amount of stress and strengthens you at the same time.

These two women, who were both highly successful in their careers, were subjected to enormous stress because of their sexual orientation. Had each been identified in their jobs as a lesbian, it may have jeopardized their positions and future opportunities. The observations of Deirdre were similar to those of other respondents who had achieved success in their careers and had to live with the threat of having an important part of themselves revealed to the world.

Deirdre went on to describe the effects on their relationship of her partner's need to remain closeted. Deirdre observed that it was "harder" for Daphne to deal with the threat of revealing her sexual identity at work. For several years, Daphne was not able to acknowledge her homosexuality publicly and to invite Deirdre to professional events. As a consequence, the sense of relatedness between them suffered, as Deirdre felt increasingly "denied" by her partner. She was expected to stay "out of view," which put great stress on their relationship. Daphne commented on her fears:

I was not out to my family. I was quite closeted, which made it very difficult for our relationship because we ended up being really the main support for each other, which was a very hard time. . . . If there was something that was going on, I probably would not go with her. I would go alone. I would go to a lot of things alone in the early years. . . . What would happen is that my partner would be denied, and that is divisive.

It was not unusual for partners, who were the "main support" for each other, to experience "agony" when their relationship could not be acknowledged in public. One felt "denied." That reaction, as Daphne observed, became divisive to the couple. Had the status quo continued, the denial and divisiveness would have eventually resulted in estrangement and, potentially, disruption of the relationship. Daphne discussed how she changed:

> Then I got fed up with that, I didn't want to do that anymore. . . . To some extent I withdrew from those kinds of situations. They weren't the kinds of situations I wanted anyway, and I began to cultivate friends and situations where we could go as partners, and I came out more. I think there is a way where both of us are accepted; at her work they are wonderfully accepting, so I would often go with her to things over the years; it was quite wonderful. She wasn't "out," but it was like they knew. . . . We all have homophobia; we are raised with it; what happens is, when one realizes that one is a lesbian, I can't accept this in me; I can't accept me; I must hide this; I must not let anybody know. One becomes not accepting of one's self. That is how I felt for years. Then, in a relationship with Deirdre, when I am being so accepted and so cared about by her and so loved by her . . . what happens is, you either have to see that for what it is or you have to devalue the person who is doing it. How can she love me? There is a way over time that acceptance from her helps me to have more acceptance, and then I think that this goes around and around and around. . . . In the relationship, there needs to be healing of the homophobia, and I think that is what has happened to me. I think Deirdre was much further ahead in all of this than I was. I've learned from her, and I think about that acceptance or that love or caring . . . then when I came out and my parents were accepting, that begins to counteract, that begins to heal the homophobic self-image, and I think that is critical.

Daphne had to weigh her fear of being open about being a lesbian with the consequences of remaining closeted, especially as the latter affected the relationship with Deirdre. She also talked of a growing awareness of her own homophobic feelings. When social and psychological homophobia were joined, as it was with Daphne, it was difficult for an individual to accept their sexual orientation as a principal component of self-identity. The experience of being in a relationship with Deirdre, who was ahead of her in accepting this part of herself, enabled Daphne to accept who she was and to dispel the negative thoughts and feelings internalized from a homophobic environment.

Another couple, Octavia and Olivia, talked of the subtle effects homophobia had on their relationship. Octavia referred to homophobia as a stressor that impacted her life and her relationship with Olivia in ways that were insidious. Octavia said that:

> I can't really put my finger on it except to say that there is something very threatening to society about us making a very good go at life without having a man. I think it is beyond what we do in bed, it is beyond being lesbians, it is the lack of being a man. I think that has really affected us. We are just not treated with respect in a lot of situations . . . it is always subtle. . . . I feel like the homophobia in society has taken away the opportunity . . . of being able to be physically intimate in public. I think that is a loss for me because I am not going to be able to change. . . . It has affected us subtly more than anything else in our workplaces. I am much more in a straight culture. Olivia works in a different culture right now. I work in an environment where the homophobia is very subtle. Sometimes I don't know it's there until years later when somebody will tell me what happened, and it had a homophobic twist to it, and I didn't even realize it. But we bring it back to our relationship . . . life is stressful, and that is an added stress. I think a lot of times we might be angry about something, and it is happening because of homophobia. We will have a fight about something else that is completely different. So I think that it is an added stress component.

The powerful yet subtle theme of social homophobia and its effect on these couples were identified by Octavia. Perhaps, as she said, homophobia may result, in part, from the meaning society assigns to women being able to survive and to prosper without being dependent on men. That message was an "added stress" on these relationships. Octavia identified a common defense that illustrated how gays and lesbians blocked out prejudicial remarks in the workplace; thus a respondent was spared the personal consequences of reacting to such remarks. Octavia also identified a way in which homophobia contaminated and increased conflicts in relationships. Her frustrations in dealing with societal constraints around homophobia and heterosexism led many times to anger and fights with Olivia around unrelated issues that were precipitated by the stress of homophobia.

Olivia commented on the effects of homophobia on their responsibilities as parents:

> We have felt pretty similar around issues of homophobia and how important it is to be out. Especially around the kids, and how

> important it is to be honest around the children and make sure they are safe. I am sure our feelings about that are pretty much the same. I may have been out earlier on than Octavia . . . there have been a lot of issues around health insurance and around the kids and all that. . . . I am sure there are things that would have been easier if we had enough acceptance like a straight couple has. . . . There are things that might have felt easier, but, you know, we are so normal. We are kind of boring, I guess. We don't really present a whole lot of challenge other than being two women; we just sort of have this normal life.

Even when partners had difficulty in coping with homophobic attitudes and practices, they expressed an obligation to be open about their sexual orientation with their children and to cultivate an atmosphere at home in which it was safe to discuss sexuality. For couples who were parents, an added stressor was social policies that excluded homosexuals from various family benefits, especially health insurance. While contending with discriminatory social policies and attitudes, lesbian parents talked like any parents about the physical and psychological well-being of their children.

INTERPERSONAL DIFFERENCES

Differences between partners always led to minor conflict and sometimes to major conflict. Age differences between partners, individual expectations of relationships, family backgrounds, and child-rearing approaches did not, in themselves, result in major conflict. Other issues that included the quality of commitment to relationships and transitions also produced conflict but did not cause serious disruptions in relationships.

When multiple differences accumulated and festered, they resulted frequently in major conflict. Differences in personal traits, sexual needs, styles of problem solving, incomes, and the management of finances contributed to major conflict. By the middle years, major conflict became a reality in about one out of two relationships.

A lesbian couple described how multiple differences between them accumulated and led to major conflict in the middle years. Although there was an abatement in major conflict during recent years, several difficulties persisted. They have been together for eighteen years. Lucy spoke of her problems with Liz:

The relationship I felt at the beginning was a kind of challenge. That might have been part of why I was attracted to her. There was something about her that was very challenging. Her emotions are quick. I'm much more laid back, much more willing to roll with the punches. . . . From her experience with her mother who babbled incessantly and being who she is, having to talk a lot all day in her work, when she gets home, she doesn't want to talk. When I get home . . . I love to just babble and babble. There is a little conflict there. . . . I'm satisfied with our life sexually, but I don't believe Liz is. She is a very good lover, and I am not sure I am a very good lover. I don't seem to be able to do the things that please her. Our way of making love is not as pleasing to her. Sometimes I don't feel Liz supports some of my desires to visit my parents or visit a friend of mine. . . . Liz admitted that she doesn't like my friend, who is very matter of fact too, like Liz. They don't always see eye to eye. Liz will say sometimes: "I wish you had as much passion about coming to see me or our spending a day together as you have when you get it into your head that you want to see your friend. You don't seem to have that much passion in you about keeping this commitment with me or about taking a day with me as you have with taking a day with her."

This excerpt illustrated how differences could result in major conflict; Lucy spoke of how complementary qualities attracted them, only to become a source of friction as the relationship unfolded. Other differences that included sexual practices, family contacts, and jealousy about relationships with friends contributed to major conflict during the middle and recent years. Unlike most couples, they were not able to find a means of resolving these problems. Interpersonal differences continued to fester into recent years.

Age differences between partners were not, in themselves, a contributor to major conflicts. An age difference could be an asset, as Liz described:

Very early on we found that when we talked to each other, the age difference simply didn't exist. I mean we understood everything the other person was saying, and I think pretty much talked on the same level. The age difference was probably good in that Lucy had already gone through a lot of the things I was going through as a young person growing up figuring out what I wanted to do with my life, what was it going to be like to be more and more responsible for myself. She wasn't as worried about those things, so it was good to be at two different parts of our lives because we didn't both have the same problems. Yet in some ways we had exactly the same problems . . . in that I don't think she'd really gone through a lot of sexual things, and I hadn't, so we kind of grew through that together. . . . When we both moved in here, it was sort of learning how to take care of a house, try to handle the checkbook, and who's going to do the dishes. . . . The only other woman I've been with is when Lucy and I were together about six years, I did have a relationship with a woman for about three-quarters of a year. I didn't leave Lucy, but she's had one and I've had one, a little one . . . to a certain extent sex is still a problem. I'd like Lucy to be more active sexually, and she's not, and that really hasn't changed, and every once in a while I get mad about it. The other issue is just differences in style of living. If I had my druthers, I usually like everything neat, everything clean, everything vacuumed, everything dusted. I don't always do that, but that's how I want it. When I decide that something's going to be clean, I clean really well! Lucy is more likely to throw stuff in a heap . . . when she tries to clean something, it's sort of clean, but it's sort of not clean. That drives me crazy, and that's been pretty consistent. Lucy sometimes spends more money than I think she should. We spend money more than save it, but I think she tends to get into bigger debts than I do. That's been a source of tension and from the beginning . . . like relationship tensions about sex . . . and my harping on her about not being as neat and clean as I'd like. It's very boring, actually. I don't think much has changed.

Communication was an important element in solving problems but was not sufficient to neutralize the development of major conflict. Openness to negotiating compromises about differences, flexibility in experimenting with alternative behaviors, and willingness to try new roles were as important as communication skills. The relationship of Lucy and Liz was characterized by an "ease" with communication but did not include behavior modifications that may have enabled them to experience higher levels of satisfaction in recent years. Similar to Lucy and Liz, several other couples had differences in sexual needs, styles of living, and managing money. Couples who did not get stuck in conflict and negotiated differences successfully were able to compromise, to be flexible in modifying their roles, and were willing to try new behaviors. Without these four elements (communication, openness, flexibility, and willingness), feelings associated with differences festered and led to severe conflict.

More than any other aspect of relationships, differences about managing finances were identified as a major conflict. This difference was more frequently reported by lesbians than by gays and usually was part of a matrix of problems that became focused on money. Liz has already commented on money as a significant contributor to major conflict in the relationship with Lucy. Pamela identified inequality of incomes as a focal point for serious conflict with Penny over the twenty years of their relationship. Recalling events during the middle years, Pamela remembered that:

> Our relationship deteriorated to arguing about money and how to spend time. It was a bad time, and there was still the stress of my not really making much money. I felt a lot of inequality around that. So I didn't want to spend money . . . she would be in tears, feeling terrible, and I would just be rational about it all . . . we could be really rigid at the time and sometimes say mean and hurtful things to each other. We would have these horrendous fights . . . about not spending enough time together. A lot of times, I would be repentant and try to get back to do my share. But I always felt this pull towards doing other things . . . even though I acknowledged this, it was very hard for me to stop doing it.

The management of money often became more of a focal point for negotiating equity, preserving autonomy within connectedness, and for resolving power and control issues. Money galvanized strong feelings associated with these relational dynamics so central to defining oneself in a relationship. For Pamela and Penny, emotions connected to managing money and "spending" time together caused distress, bitterness, and chronic tensions that resulted in destructive fights. From observing their efforts, Pamela became aware of the injuries that bitter words inflicted on Penny. Each partner was open to modifying her behavior and trying less hurtful ways of expressing anger after becoming aware that expressing "horrible things to each other was really injuring." The shift in role behaviors that included milder language to express anger led to a higher level of adaptation in recent years.

As their relationship changed, this couple decided to become parents, which introduced further stress into the relationship. After working for years to reach a mutually satisfying level of intimacy, their privacy was compromised as children "came between" them, and they "again questioned whether we could stay together because it was so difficult." Because of the relational work that had been accomplished, they were able to adapt to the "watershed" of becoming parents. The gains in the development of their communication skills, along with openness, flexibility, and willingness to modify behaviors, were invaluable resources as Pamela and Penny integrated the role of parenthood into their relationship. In reflecting on that process, Pamela observed:

> I don't consider myself a totally different person. . . . I feel that we are better now and that has taken a long time to start seeing how the other person feels; you have to say what's really bothering you. . . . I tend to want to move faster than Penny . . . she tends to brood about it, and I have to say: "Okay, what's bothering you?"

As she thought back to the early years, Penny's memories of conflict were similar to those of Pamela:

> In the early days, most of our difficulties centered around money and time—the amount of time we each gave to the relationship and then later on the issue of children. But those two things, money and time, plagued us for a really long time. Pamela was involved in political activities, and I felt those things taking over our time together. The issue of money was I would spend too much, and Pamela was too reticent to spend it. We have always had problems around that.
>
> I think when we first started realizing that those things were serious was when we were buying a house, and all the things came up about money; my sort of being more impulsive . . . that triggered Pamela being more involved in her activities outside of our house; it was more pleasant because at home we were always fighting. I started spending more time at home watching TV and totally involved in thinking that I had to keep this relationship together. So we decided to go into therapy, and that was a very good experience. It started out as a sort of useless experience because we would go to therapy each week and tell the therapist the fights we had over and over and over. Nothing was changing. One day we went in, and our therapist said: "Well, you have to make a decision. Either you want this relationship or not." It really jolted me.

An important aspect of the relationships of couples in the study was the similarity in the observations of partners about conflict over the years, even when conflict became severe as it did between Pamela and

Penny. As feelings about differences in spending habits became in-flamed and led to nasty fights, Pamela withdrew from the relationship by involvement in community activities. Despite the estrangement chronic fighting had caused, they struggled to cope with their difficul-ties. Only after it became apparent that the estrangement would result in a separation did they seek professional help. Interestingly, the therapist's intervention, that they had to decide whether they wanted to remain together or not, appeared to be a turning point in their relationship. They learned new ways of managing conflict and acquired skills in identifying feelings, expressing them with appropriate language rather than through hurtful fights, and demonstrated a willingness to try new modes of solving problems. Rather than weapons, words now became tools for work toward higher levels of relatedness. Although fights continued, especially about child rearing, they became less frequent and interchanges were less destructive. They developed ob-servational skills to identify flashpoints that led to anger and came to know when further discussion served no constructive purpose. They learned to disengage from these potential powder kegs and to return later to a dialogue when the emotional flame had subsided.

MANAGING CONFLICT

We asked respondents to describe how they and their partners dealt with conflict. Based on what respondents reported, we conceptualized a continuum of predominant modes of conflict management behavior, with avoidance at one pole and confrontation at the other. Avoidance included any defensive maneuvers to deny or to escape face-to-face discussion of conflict. Confrontation included any effort to express one's thoughts and feelings directly to the partner in a face-to-face encounter.

Figure 5.2 shows the patterns of avoidance of conflict over the years. Substantial numbers of respondents in each group managed conflict by avoidance, especially during the early and middle years. A majority of gay and lesbian partners utilized avoidant styles early in the relationship, a pattern that increased slightly among gays during the middle years when it declined among lesbians. During recent years, a majority of respondents described confrontative means of dealing with conflict. Among lesbians, a progressive pattern of using face-to-face modes of dealing with conflict replaced avoidant modes.

Figure 5.2
Avoidant Style of Managing Conflict between Partners

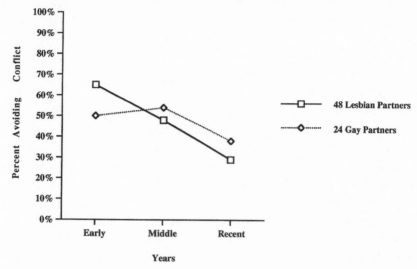

There were qualitative differences between the two groups in handling conflict. Gays tended to deal with major conflict only when relationships were at risk. As long as relationships were without significant disruptions, most gays avoided face-to-face discussions of conflict. They often talked about going along with their partners or making compromises with little discussion of their feelings about basic differences. Many lesbians used their communication and conversational skills to avoid potentially powerful feelings during the early and middle years of relationships. As we have already pointed out in discussing decision-making styles, lesbian partners were adept in processing their experiences; they invested considerable effort into talking about and understanding what had happened between them. Often, however, they avoided powerful feelings associated with interpersonal conflict.

There were several dynamics associated with the avoidant behaviors between partners; they included:

1. fear of abandonment
2. not knowing how to fight
3. similarity to parents who used avoidant behaviors
4. shame and guilt about aggressive feelings
5. fear of losing control

6.   expecting a partner to know how one feels and thinks

A major dynamic that led to avoidant behavior was a fear of abandonment by the partner as a consequence of expressing aggression. Several respondents talked of their anticipation of destroying relationships by driving a partner away if they openly said how they felt. That irrational yet common fear was evident as Beverly spoke about her partner's fear of being abandoned:

> Betsy learned somewhere that if you're that angry with somebody, you didn't love them. I kept saying I love you just as much even if I'm furious at you. I don't want to leave you. I think she would be afraid that I was going to leave. I think I had been much more secure in her love than she has been in mine . . . she thought I would leave her.

Another dynamic that shaped the use of avoidant defenses was that partners did not know, nor had they ever learned, how to confront conflict. This lack of skill in contending with conflict in a face-to-face way was triggered often by anxiety about abandonment or losing control. Isabelle spoke to the theme of learning how to deal with conflict when she observed that:

> In the beginning, we argued less and probably communicated less. We still got along fine. We were just quite compatible . . . there was lots that we did talk about, but in terms of our relationship, we each had a life that we didn't share with each other, and then we started to talk a little bit about it. That was a hard thing for us, because neither of us were used to tolerating the tension and discomfort if there was a disagreement or anything like that. . . . I think that it's gotten better with each segment of time. That's still something that we work on . . . we don't thrive on arguments, but we reluctantly understand that you have to do that sometimes. You have to disagree. We just have to discuss when there is disagreement.

Psychotherapy appeared to be a valuable resource that offered partners tools and skills in learning how to discuss feelings and deal with conflict in a confrontative yet constructive way. An important element in not knowing how to fight was the social context in which gays and lesbians lived. When they were the victims of discrimination or prejudice, many gays and lesbians adopted avoidant behaviors to deal with homophobic threat. Avoidance of feelings associated with unpleasant social situations often carried over to relationships with partners.

The internalized qualities of important role models, particularly parents who were avoidant in dealing with conflict in their relationships, was a third element tht shaped avoidance. Many respondents talked about how they were similar to a parent who had dealt with feelings, especially angry ones, by avoiding face-to-face discussion. Although they did not like how their parents handled conflict, they internalized a parent's way of dealing with feelings about conflict. Jennifer spoke of how she and her partner adopted parental ways of dealing with aggression:

> My anger and Joyce's withdrawal have been what we fight about . . . she's pulled back and not talking and I'm bitching and moaning. . . . We know what the issue is. I had a withdrawn mother, and she had an angry mother; so we know what that's about, but we just sometimes still do it.

Personal problems contributed to avoidant behaviors in some relationships. This was particularly true of partners who were impaired cognitively and emotionally because of phobias, depression, or substance abuse. Psychological impairments contributed to cognitive blocks in identifying feelings and expressing them to partners. The process fed on itself, so that the impaired individuals withdrew more and more from communicating with their partners. Their withdrawal created serious obstacles in dealing with conflict. Unless the unimpaired partner broke the cycle of despair, withdrawal, and estrangement, patterns of avoidance were not likely to change. Beverly described how she broke through Betsy's avoidance by telling her how upset she was:

> She's had a couple of very bad depressions, and just before I was able to get her to therapy we had some really hard times. I was so frustrated with her. . . . I didn't know what to do . . . the only way I could figure out how to get her there was to show her how upset I was. Finally, when I showed her how upset I was, she'd finally say, "OK," and she would trot along to therapy.

Resentment and anger toward a partner generated guilt, which prevented individuals from being assertive about their anger in a contained and appropriate way and led to avoidant behavior. This pattern was true even among respondents who maintained highly adaptive styles of functioning with partners in other aspects of their relationships, and among individuals who functioned well in friendships and work-related roles. The more anger was repressed, the more it created serious secondary effects and prevented individuals from facing original feelings of resentment and anger toward their partner. The need to control angry feelings fed on itself, so that individuals became increasingly more fearful of expressing even understandable and appropriate feelings to a partner. The underlying dynamics in this insidious process was that individuals became progressively more fearful that their aggressive feelings, if expressed to the partners, would lead to terrible consequences. These consequences included a fear that the relationship would end or that the partner would abandon them.

A final source of avoidant behavior was found among a few individuals who expressed the expectation of entitlement of understanding without having to let the partner know of their feelings. For these individuals, needing to communicate to the partner what their needs were was an indication that the partner really did not care about them. Had partners "really" cared, they would have been able to "read one's mind" and understand their partner's feelings. The hurt experienced by the perception of a partner's failure to be sensitive to one's hidden feelings reinforced avoidant patterns of behavior.

AVOIDANCE OF CONFRONTATION

There was considerable modification in these relationships in modes of dealing with conflict that enabled partners to develop more mature levels of relatedness during recent years. Partners moved from less to more adaptive modes of dealing with conflict as they developed skills in expressing thoughts and feelings about differences directly to their partners. These elements included:

1. accepting differences
2. learning how to confront constructively
3. lessening of abandonment anxiety
4. learning to express needs
5. mutual and reciprocal modifications in avoidant behaviors
6. compromise
7. letting go and moving on

One of the more profound elements in understanding change toward adaptive functioning was in the acceptance of fundamental differences between partners. When partners were able to acknowledge difficulties between them and experienced understanding and respect for the "way they were," acceptance of differences became a reality; they stopped trying to change partners. Fundamental to acceptance was understanding. Once partners understood why they behaved as they did, self-acceptance followed; once they understood why their partners behaved as they did, they were able to accept them. Understanding had a neutralizing effect on anger in contrast to behavioral maneuvers aimed at manipulating partners into changing themselves. Grace comments on the impact on their relationship of mutual acceptance:

> We just found ourselves oppositional a lot. Feeling polarized very quickly over the words, you would say. Is this half full or half empty used to be one of our real phrases. Are we looking at this half full or half empty? We would just be aware that we start at different places. She would do the work first and the fun later. I would want to have fun first and do the work later . . . if we hadn't talked about it, we would have had totally different ideas about what it would actually be . . . there is always a shock to find somebody that looks at the world like you, and she doesn't look at anything like you.

A second aspect of change was in partners learning how to confront each other in constructive ways. Ways of confrontation varied from calm face-to-face discussions of thoughts and feelings to clean yet spirited fights. In order to integrate within themselves confrontative rather than avoidant modes of dealing with thoughts and feelings about conflict, partners needed to reach mutual acceptance of differences. A renewed sense of connection based on mutual acceptance, understanding, and caring between partners was essential for them to incorporate face-to-face ways of dealing with conflict into their relationships. Gwen speaks about these themes:

> In some way we stopped fighting each other a while back in a good way. . . . I can see more the value of her way, and she can see the value of my way, so that we are not just in opposite corners quite as much . . . basic differences . . . don't get resolved. I think a lot of it is that you resolve what you can and what you can carry on. I'm an introvert; Grace is an extrovert. That is never going to

change. I think, and she feels. We approach things in a different way . . . therapy let us see how we truly are different, and you don't have to try to change the other person.

Another element in understanding modifications of behaviors was the experience, cognitively and emotionally, of discovering that confrontation did not lead to abandonment. As partners were able to express their feelings about conflict without having their worst fears realized, they were able to build on the initial confrontative steps they had taken. Emily, who has been with Elaine for twenty years, spoke on that theme:

During the first seven or eight years we were together, the one thing I was afraid of the most was that she would leave me if I did something that displeased her. . . . I remember the worst fight we ever had at that time; we could have split up. The fact that we didn't gave me the confidence to be able to disagree . . . that was a big transition: that we can actually disagree and have a knock-down-drag-out and still stay together . . . it's important, I think, to be able to fight fairly.

A fourth aspect in understanding change was that people learned not only how to confront constructively, but how to make their needs known to their partners. The impediment toward expressing needs was often based on feelings of shame and guilt about selfishness. Many individuals did not feel entitled to be treated in the way they wished. At the same time, when needs for understanding, acceptance, and love were not acknowledged and validated, partners became resentful, withdrew, and avoided putting their needs into words. As they became able to risk letting their partners know their needs, relationships improved and became more satisfying. Deirdre discussed how individual impairments obscured talking with her partner about her inner needs:

I don't think that at the beginning we ever fought . . . part of the reason for that was underneath it all I was angry because I wasn't having my needs met. Why should I, because I never made them known? I was drinking a great deal more, and so I could blow up and get explosive and have a reason or what I thought was an excuse at that time. . . . For a while there I started to rebel. I refused to sit and talk about another single thing. What Daphne was learning through her therapy was to actually make her needs known. We got into this little ritual: "There is something I need to talk to you about." We would come in here, and Daphne would sit there, and I would sit here, and it was like having a session of some sort.

One of the primary reasons for these relationships lasting was in the mutual and reciprocal nature of behavioral modifications. Had only one partner modified behavior, it would have left the other partner behind developmentally. A result may have been an increased estrangement and the potential end of the relationship. This was evident as Deirdre talked about the mutuality of modifications in the relationship with Daphne. She had been saying that "real open communication" had not been part of their relationship until recent years and then described the "work" that each of them did to reach a higher level of relatedness:

I did my emotional work. Daphne did a tremendous amount of emotional work. She is a totally different person. I think I am different also, but . . . I still have trouble with communication . . . so it is a struggle . . . we owe a lot to Daphne's patience and willingness to take small steps at a time and to let me know exactly where she stands; that forces me to identify what is going on with me . . . she was extremely clear where she is at any given moment. She keeps giving me a verbal model of ways of saying it. It really helped me through. Now I know what is going on with me.

Compromise was an essential ingredient in the process of modifying behaviors and in developing equity between partners. Compromise represented many important dynamics in relationships, not the least of which was mutual caring and commitment. To compromise was a statement that one not only cared about the relationship but represented a commitment to stay in the relationship and to work toward more adaptive modes of dealing with conflict. Gary and George spoke about the process of compromise. Gary said:

I would say: "Try to understand, even if I'm wrong, this is the way I'm feeling. If I'm wrong, you can say so." But that's pretty much it. He's gotten a lot better too. We're both a lot better at compromising. We really are. . . . I'm here and I'm giving one hundred percent, one hundred and twenty or thirty percent, and he's doing the same; we have to listen to each other. We've gotten to a point now where we do.

George described the evolution of their relationship, which included a mutual willingness to compromise in recent years:

> We're both very nonconfrontational people. But on other levels it's hard because if there's a problem we don't want to confront . . . that can be hard. . . . At the beginning, it was: "Anything you want, darling." There were no conflicts because we were perfect. . . . The second five years . . . there was a lot more conflict. I was trying to find who I was in the relationship . . . the last five years the conflicts are negotiated. We work on it together, and sometimes somebody gives in, and sometimes we negotiate the decisions.

As partners negotiated less avoidant and more confrontative ways of dealing with conflict, they were able to let go of the past and move on to a more mature relational plateau. To reach this state, partners needed to experience a genuine sense of mutual acceptance in the relationship as well as an understanding of each other's needs and feelings. The mutuality of acceptance and understanding allowed partners to integrate new modes of conflict management into their relationship.

SUMMARY

Conflict based on differences between partners was inevitable given the high levels of complementarity in their relationships. When partners avoided confronting differences about sex, money, individual temperaments, traits, and expectations, the unresolved differences often resulted in major conflict. Compared to minor or everyday conflict, which was inevitable in these relationships, major conflict was highly distressing to partners and had a significant disruptive effect on their relationships. The most stressful times were during the middle years when major conflict was reported by more than half of all respondents. Major conflict resulted in a decline in physical and psychological intimacy and undermined mutual trust, respect, and understanding.

Differences were apparent between gays and lesbians in how they spoke about major conflict. More lesbians than gays reported major conflict throughout their relationships, which may have reflected the orientation of women to discuss relational matters more than men. The propensity of women to process their experiences may have resulted in more frequent identification of conflict between lesbian partners compared to gay partners. Perhaps in their relational orientation to life, women were more accepting of the presence of serious conflict. As relationships evolved from beginning to recent years, lesbians became less avoidant in dealing with thoughts and feelings about conflict than did gays.

In their initial response to conflict, more than six out of ten respondents avoided face-to-face discussion during the early years, which declined to three out of ten respondents in recent years. Dynamics associated with avoidant styles of managing conflict included fear of losing relationships if feelings about differences were confronted, insecurities about losing control, and never having learned how to fight in a fair and contained way. Several respondents saw themselves as not being able to change avoidant styles they saw as similar to their parents'.

As partners negotiated their ways through relationships, they developed adaptive modes of dealing with conflict and handling differences. For many couples, psychotherapy focused on relational problems was a valuable resource for work on personal differences and helping couples move to a higher developmental plateau. Most commonly, respondents learned to accept fundamental differences within themselves and in their partners that were not going to change. At the same time, they were able to develop skills to confront their differences. Integrating acceptance and confrontation promoted modifications in relational behaviors such as compromise, articulating needs, and communication skills. Partners were then free to let go of the past and to move on to a more satisfying relationship.

6

Intimacy

It's more and more a meshing of two spirits.

Relational intimacy was characterized by and nurtured through the mutual sense of communion between partners in the physical, emotional, and intellectual dimensions of their shared lives. Understood in this way, intimacy between partners changed as these relationships evolved from early to recent years. Psychological intimacy progressed over the years. Respondents talked about experiencing psychological intimacy when they were able to share their inner thoughts and feelings that were accepted, if not understood, by the partner. Sexual intimacy moved in a regressive direction, while the physical expression of affection, such as touching and hugging, remained constant from early through recent years. In this chapter, we explore the quality of sexual and psychological intimacy as well as the physical expression of affection.

SEXUAL INTIMACY

Sexual intimacy was defined as genital sexual relations. Genital sex was different from the physical expression of affection, such as hugging, and did not necessarily involve the same level of interpersonal closeness as did psychological intimacy. Sexual relations were a barometer of psychological intimacy early in relationships and also served to nurture, reassure, and strengthen the quality of relationships. The quality of sexual intimacy included both the frequency of sexual relations and how satisfying sex was for respondents. In figure 6.1 the patterns of sexual intimacy are shown. Although the frequency and satisfaction with sexual relations was slightly higher among gays compared with lesbians, there was an overall decline in sexual intimacy for all respondents from early to recent years. We chose excerpts from interviews with a gay and a lesbian couple to illustrate that decline. Daniel observed that:

> Dwight has always been what I consider more sexual than I have . . . between the two of us, he's more sexual, and I tend to be less sexual. So there's a constant struggle to make each person get what they need, but that doesn't make it a threat to the relationship . . . he's not going to leave me. We've gone beyond that phase . . . it's an issue that we need to work on, an important issue, but it's not going to separate us . . . initially, it was very physical . . . the love certainly developed after that. Now we're in a phase where again we have some sexual issues. They're difficult to deal with, because Dwight is a romantic at heart, and

Figure 6.1
Positive Sexual Relations between Partners

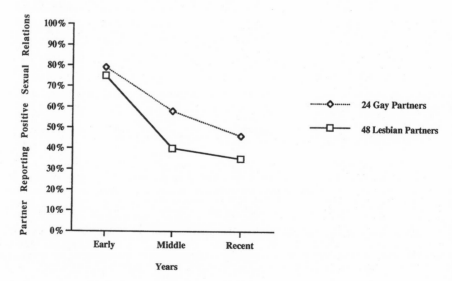

> he wants to believe that it's always going to be like the day we met, and that we're going to really want each other that lustfully and we're going to be that attracted to each other. For me it's not that way. . . . It's not a real important part of my relationship. I like sex but with age you perform less adequately, or you have a bad week, or you're stressed from work, or whatever it is . . . he is more concerned about the fact that we are progressively having less sex than I am.

The observations of Daniel were typical of those we heard from many respondents. An important aspect of sexual intimacy was in the differing needs of partners. More than any other potential problem in the sexual dimension of their lives together was the difference in sexual needs, which was the focus of negotiations from the beginning of relationships to the present time.

Another theme identified frequently by all respondents was the interrelationship of sexual and psychological intimacy. As genital sex became less frequent and satisfying in recent years, the quality of the relationships became increasingly important. Daniel commented on that trend when he observed:

> At this point in my life, I feel that my love for him and my desire to be with him is much more important . . . we're going through a normal thing in life where it's nicer to cuddle together at night than to do it. . . . For him it's an important thing that my desires for him physically have lessened. . . . I don't see it as a threat to the marriage; I don't see my leaving him and having extramarital affairs. I don't have a desire for that . . . it's hard because I understand what he's saying; it's important to show your love and feelings for people, but on the other hand, if you're feeling forced into a situation, then it's not going to be healthy or positive.

Differences, such as those identified by Daniel, became focal issues between partners as they struggled to adapt to individual differences in sexual drives and needs. Another challenge for Daniel was in articulating his love for his partner. He felt that he had always experienced difficulty in expressing his love with words. As Daniel's interest in sexual relations waned, Dwight began to question the love his partner had for him, particularly as sexual relations had been a means through which Daniel communicated his love.

From Dwight's perspective, he remembered sexual relations during the early years as "spectacular," followed by declining frequency and satisfaction during the middle years. In recent years, Dwight said that:

> Sex has become more work . . . neither one of us are as sexual towards each other. But I think it's an important part of a relationship, and we have to work on it . . . compared to the beginning when sex was paramount . . . now, things have, as we've gotten older, flipped around a little bit, where although I still absolutely believe you can't ignore sex; it has to be an important part of the relationship, but it is definitely not as important as it was.

Many respondents made observations similar to those of Dwight about aging and sexual relations. They wondered, as he did, if "people become less sexual as they became older." Yet respondents did not consider sex as any less important as they aged. In fact, the importance of sex remained constant throughout the years, with more than 70 percent of all respondents saying that sexual relations were important to the viability of their relationships. During recent years when sexual intimacy had reached its lowest point, 92 percent of gays and 71 percent of lesbians reported that sex was important to relationships. During that same period of time, only 46 percent of gays and 35 percent of lesbians were satisfied with their sexual relations. Given these discrepancies between the realities of sexual relations and their importance, the challenge of adaptation was a significant one.

A lesbian couple spoke on the theme of decline in sexual intimacy. Angela recalled:

> When we first made love together . . . it just felt so right, so natural, so happy, and so wonderful. I didn't understand why I had been so scared for such a long time . . . initially, we couldn't keep our hands off each other, but that's very much like any newlywed people . . . it's been less frequent in the middle and in this later time. . . . It seems to come in waves. Sometimes there's like a dry spell for a period of time, and then sometimes you know I look at her as if I haven't seen her before. Something very new, and I just feel in love with her all over again. It surprises me, and I love it . . . she says she feels very much the same way . . . the quality of our being together sexually is different now.

Although the frequency of sexual relations between these partners lessened, they did not experience a corresponding decrease in satisfaction as was reported by many couples. The "dry spells" may have been more frequent and longer than they had been earlier in the relationship, but the satisfaction with sex remained strong, at least with Angela. Her need for sex did not wane as it had for Daniel.

Alice had enjoyed sexual relations with men before meeting Angela. She, too, remembered the beginning of their relationship as a novel experience and described its meaning to her in the following way:

> When we made love, it felt so natural. It was like, I'm home! I'm home! This is where I want to be. It was so wonderful to be with a woman. I really had enjoyed being with men, too. It wasn't like it was better, but it was different. But I really, really loved Angela, and I waited. It sounds like a commercial for teenagers who should wait until they're married before having sex, but it is. It's very powerful to finally give yourself in that way.

Remembering the first time when they were together sexually, Alice reported:

> That first night it wasn't great sex in terms of any kind of technique, because I didn't know what to do exactly. I was afraid. . . . It was just the emotions and the feeling; I woke up in the morning and I just went: I am so happy; I just love this woman. There was more sex in the beginning. That sort of slowly diminishes until you get into more of a pattern of fewer times. It's still really good and an important part of our lives. It hasn't stopped, which is really nice.

Alice went on to place sexual intimacy within the context of the relationship as a whole. Although men may have also thought of sex in a similar way, women were more likely to comment explicitly on the significance of sexual relations as a manifestation of the quality of their relationships. Alice said of sex:

> It's really connecting. I think the only thing is that I wish it was a little more often, because there are times when I want to, but I think we have the same problem a lot of people do. Sometimes we're too tired.

Decline in sexual intimacy was also affected by factors other than physical limitations associated with aging, which were mentioned by

Daniel and Dwight as well as Angela and Alice. The presence of children among those couples who were parents, and historical experiences such as incest and highly repressive family attitudes about open discussion of sexuality, were identified as important in understanding sexual intimacy. Beatrice talked of how sexual intimacy had changed over the years. Both partners had previous heterosexual relationships and met after Barbara had been married for several years and was the mother of three children. Beatrice spoke about how their being busy parents as well as her history of incest affected sexual intimacy with Barbara. She began by observing how her sexual drive, which she felt was strong in the early years of their relationship, had changed:

> In terms of sexual intimacy, I would say in the first seven years it was very intense. After that, it really slacked off. I had never had a sexual relationship before in my life. Barbara had, but it had been very fraught with a lot of pain . . . she wasn't fitting the heterosexual mode much better than I was. There were the three kids, and there wasn't a lot of time to be private. In the last seven years we hardly have any sexual intimacy to speak of at all. We have talked about it some. It has been more painful for me than it has for Barbara. For me, part of it is related to the incest I experienced, and it has been helpful for me to understand that. For her, I think, part of it is she went through menopause early because of a surgery she had. So she never really had a strong sexual drive to begin with, and it is less now. She lived with a man who was very gentle who never forced her or anything but had a normal male sexual drive. But they didn't have the emotional intimacy that went with it, so for her that was a very uncomfortable and unwelcoming expectation. On some level, I still think she is perhaps enjoying being able to be sexual but not having genital sex. In other words, being able to enjoy the freedom of not having that expectation . . . that is where we are at now.

The decline of sexual intimacy was described by Barbara:

> In terms of genital sexual expression, in the beginning we were very active and for quite a number of years. I think Beatrice has had more of a sex drive in general, and that has been a cause of a lot of discussion between us, especially in recent years. I would say maybe in the past four or five years there has been a decline. I don't need to be genitally sexually active as much as she does. We talked a lot about that in terms of what does that

mean, what does that say about our relationship? Of course the usual question that arises: don't I love her? So, we spend a lot of time talking about that; I don't know if we have come up with any great answers. I don't think we have made love genitally in about eight months. For me, I am not missing that. That is not a problem for me. We haven't had a very recent conversation about it, so I don't know if right now it is a problem with her or not. But it is something we discussed a lot. For me, genital sex has a lot to do with energy level, and at my particular age I struggle with my energy level. In my mind it sounds like a great idea, and in my fantasy it sounds like a wonderful thing to be doing, but in reality I am dead.

All couples had to contend with several factors that shaped the frequency of and satisfaction with sexual relations over the years. The effects of aging including menopause, parental responsibilities, and histories of sexual abuse were identified by several respondents as contributing to declining sexual intimacy. Rarely, however, were there so many factors present in the experiences of partners as there were in the lives of Beatrice and Barbara.

PHYSICAL AFFECTION

Compared with sexual intimacy, the expression of affection through physical touching and hugging without genital sex remained, more or less, constant from the early years to the present, although there was a decline in physical intimacy in the middle years. Physically expressing affection to partners was reported by more than 70 percent of respondents during early and recent years. In the middle years when relationships became more conflictual than at any other period, 67 percent of gays and 58 percent of lesbians engaged in touching and hugging their partners.

Expressing affection physically was a characteristic individuals brought with them into relationships that was acquired through identification with role models. If respondents came from families in which important figures expressed their affection for others through physical contact, individuals were likely to use similar means to express their feelings to their partners. For example, Jeffrey, after saying that physical intimacy was "a big part of our life," talked of his father as a "hugger, so hugging was important to me." Jeffrey went on to describe how his father hugged everybody and remembered him as "a very warm, loving man. . . . I've always wanted to be like my father." Expressing affection through hugging and touching was similar to other traits that had become part of oneself. Not uncommonly, individuals who were not as demonstrative in expressing their affections were attracted to individuals like Jeffrey.

Physical intimacy was a visible and reassuring manifestation of expressing basic human needs for spiritual connection with another human being whom one loved. Alice talked of this exigency when she observed that bodily contact was "a human need to be near someone, to be touching." Commenting on the evolution of the relationship with her partner, she made the analogy to husbands and wives in heterosexual relationships who "end up more like a brother and a sister. . . . I think in some ways that we've melded more into a sensual relationship; sexual more in the beginning and now sensual." As couples grew older, physical closeness without genital sexual relations became increasingly meaningful to these relationships.

Despite the prevalence of physical intimacy, several couples did not see themselves needing to express their connection with each other in this way. Deirdre reported, "I don't need to feel close to her physically in order to feel close to her." Her partner felt differently, observing, "I still want more touching than she does. . . . It is a way that I feel reassured." When partners had different needs for expressing and receiving physical expressions of affection, it was important for them to discuss their differences. Understanding and accepting these differences was critical to the well-being of relationships, because this was an individual trait not likely to change appreciably over the years.

A "U"-shaped pattern to physical intimacy over the years in most relationships was described by a gay partner. During the early years he remembered physical intimacy as "hot and happening. It was nice to be there. . . . It was just touching, an emotional bond; it was a constant affectionate attention, the touching, hand holding, arms around each other." During the middle years this dimension of their relationship changed dramatically and was associated with major conflict between them. He said that physical intimacy "died" at that time. In recent years, "it blossomed again. Not sexual, but it's physical, touching, warm and friendly . . . an arm around the shoulder . . . is really more important than sex, I think." The observations of this man resonated with those of other respondents. For partners who were accustomed to expressing affection in this way, physical intimacy was an indicator of how they felt about their relationships at various times. Withdrawing physically was a sign of interpersonal trouble, not unlike prolonged silences.

HIV/AIDS

HIV has an enormous impact on both homosexual and heterosexual relationships. The lethal nature of the virus along with its insidious behavior has created apprehension and dread among individuals and couples who are sexually active. The virus had a significant effect on couples in this study, particularly on the sexual practices of gay couples. For those couples who practiced sexual monogamy, HIV had a reinforcing effect on that decision. For some gay couples who had an open sexual relationship, HIV and the threat of infection led to the adoption of a monogamous lifestyle. For others, it made them cautious about engaging in sexual practices that put them at risk for becoming infected.

In this section we are the conduit for telling the story of one couple's encounter with HIV. The voices of Keith and Ken tell of their initial reactions to the news over ten years ago that Ken was infected and of the discovery eighteen months later that Keith was also infected. They spoke of how the quality of their commitment to each other enabled them to weather the trauma of hearing the lethal news. Their initial reactions, which lasted a few years, were followed by a period of acceptance of the reality they faced together. The question marks on the horizons of their existence enabled them to sort through the priorities of their lives. Part of that process was accepting the pain that dreams for their future would never become real, particularly the dream to have children. After ten years of living with the virus, Keith and Ken were reconciled to the fate of living their lives without knowing what the future will hold.

In their individual interviews, Keith and Ken were talking about developments in their relationship ten years before when Ken was diagnosed with HIV. Keith speaks first:

> The other big, sort of watershed in the mid-eighties was that we discovered that Ken was HIV positive. It took me a long time to get over it because it was a loaded, cocked gun, a death sentence. We scrambled around doing all sorts of things . . . we went to the insurance agent, we had to write wills; we had a lawyer, and got involved in how do you keep yourself healthy for the long term. That was an intense period of time, and we relied on each other a lot, and we talked about everything: maybe we shouldn't do this; maybe we shouldn't do that; maybe we should just lose our deposit on the house and not add the stress of having

to make financial commitments; maybe we should do something different. HIV, I think, really pushed us together. There was never a thought in my mind that what we were going to do was to see it through. The experience changed us, cemented us together . . . we became adults. We didn't have an inkling about HIV. We didn't know about me, but I simply assumed that if Ken was positive, I must be positive too. I didn't get tested for another year and a half . . . the positive results didn't surprise me. I had been sort of prepared for it because I believed in my heart what the situation was.

Keith talked of their initial flurry of activity in reacting to the news of Ken's infection. The dread of anticipating that he, too, was infected pushed him to avoid HIV testing for a year and a half. An invaluable resource to both partners during those traumatic years was the solidarity of their relationship based on their mutual commitment.

Ken spoke of his reactions to the news of being infected with HIV:

The other thing that is significant was finding out that I'm HIV positive . . . if I was HIV positive there was no way, unless there was some amazing miracle, that Keith wasn't HIV positive, given behaviors. That's a significant thing, both in terms of personal concerns and relationship concerns. We certainly had been, for the years prior to then, each other's primary emotional support network. This only made it more so. In the mid-eighties, the knowledge that one was HIV positive didn't tell you much. It told you that . . . you just didn't know. You could be dead in six months; you could be nothing; there wasn't much to do at that point; there wasn't AZT yet, and there weren't any anti-viral therapies. It was a big question mark.

No doubt, Ken mirrored his partner's fear that Keith was also infected. In addition to the news was the reality of the state of knowledge about HIV and AIDS in the mid-1980s. He knew only of being sick with a deadly disease but not of its prognosis. There was little treatment available, a reality extremely difficult to integrate, especially in view of the deadly nature of the virus and the unknown life expectancy of its victim. Ken spoke of the importance of the relationship with Keith, the primary source of emotional support in contending with his fate.

This couple had many friends but felt relatively isolated after Ken was diagnosed and even more cut off from friends and family after Keith's diagnosis. Keith talked of how the strength each partner derived from their relationship freed them to reach out to others and take a new step in adapting to their illness:

> We needed to talk to somebody. We told one other couple, but we didn't tell our families for a long time. . . . I feel like it drove us together; I don't mean that in a negative way. It made life so clear that we wanted and had to be there for each other. The absolute total commitment to this relationship was never questioned after that. . . . I still sort of can't fathom when people find out they're HIV positive or have AIDS and take off. It's really just not in me, and I know it's not in Ken. I feel like, if there's any positive thing that could come from HIV, it has put us together and made us very clear about the priorities, and about the priority of the relationship, which was not something that was a being unto itself. It was sort of his, mine, and ours. It's mostly ours now; his health is important to me, and my health is important to him . . . all that is so wrapped up together that I can't conceive of an alternative to this arrangement. It is the right thing for my heart, for my mind, for my body; this is the person that I want to be with. . . . I feel like we're still in that same phase that started back then, and that it's just grown over the intervening ten years. . . . We've broken the statistic already. This is our tenth-year anniversary of the HIV, and we're both asymptomatic . . . we don't want to disrupt anything, and we keep going. Health concerns were probably on the forefront of our minds and unspoken, because we didn't know what to do with it. And then the last five years it has been easier for us to talk about things and to make mutual decisions and . . . not keep it to oneself, but just to say: "I think I need to call my doctor"; as opposed to: "If I don't say anything, maybe it will just go away." In a nutshell, I think it represents the relationship; in those five years we sort of tiptoed around each other a little bit in some ways, because we didn't want to upset anything. And then in the last five years it's been that we can talk about issues.

Both partners took steps toward engaging their mutual foe and moved beyond their initial reactions to the trauma. The mutuality that had characterized their relationship was strengthened as they struggled to adapt to the reality of living with a new horizon in view. Their commitment to living out their remaining years together, no matter how many years remained, was renewed. The quality of their friendship and the mutual support the relationship offered were invaluable resources in confronting the terror they had struggled to deny.

Ken commented on their efforts to integrate the reality of HIV infection into their lives and to live as each partner wished:

> One assumes at our age, you've got a fairly distant horizon. The one thing that it did, in terms of the way that you look at your life, is: "Gee, that horizon may not be that far away. The horizon may be closer than it used to be." It caused one to go through a major reevaluation of what's important in your life. Something everybody could say at that point was to at least work on reducing stress in your life; we think there might be some correlation between stress and progression of HIV into AIDS . . . so we sort of very quickly separated the wheat from the chaff, what was important and what was not important. Our love for each other was of primary importance, and the life that we were building together was important. . . . One of the significant changes in my thoughts about what would happen in the next years of our life was, all of a sudden, raising children . . . that was cut out as an option, with the question mark of the horizon, and now it's ten years later. Keeping on and keeping on, and what's happened over time is that someplace, about four years ago, the horizon started to move out again . . . here I am, still as healthy as I was in 1985. My medical provider can't explain it; medicine can't explain it, not with any degree of certainty. Being in the gay community, I see people who appear to be as healthy as I was at the beginning who I watch get sicker and die, but yet that's not happening to me. We've lost a number of very good friends, and here we are still healthy. There used to be some guilt about it, but I can't be guilty about that. I'm thankful and happy, and whatever we're doing, we're doing it right, and whether it's a less virulent strain of HIV, or the lack or re-exposure, or whatever, I didn't think in the mid-eighties that I'd be sitting here today. Maybe it's another three years, maybe it's five years, maybe it's ten years, maybe we're going to live to be eighty-five.

One of the tragedies of living with HIV was in accepting that at least some dreams would never become a reality. Indeed, the dream of becoming a parent could no longer be enjoyed even as a dream because of the intrusiveness of HIV. Adaptation, so clearly articulated in what Keith and Ken said, was the capacity to live with the disappointments of dreams unfulfilled and to find a reason for living despite the loss.

The relationship of this couple provided a buffer to absorb the shock of that loss. For Ken the potential of HIV progressing into AIDS surrounded him and was a constant reminder of the tragedy in his life with Keith. We wonder how he and his partner would have coped with the tragedy of their lives had they not had a loving relationship that helped to contain their mutual grief.

In a final passage from the interview with Keith, he talked of reconciliation and the absence of recrimination for the presence of HIV in their lives:

I think one of the things I use as a benchmark of our relationship was that we have never dwelt on who brought HIV into this house. We both did the same things over the same period of time and with the same ignorance, and it doesn't matter. It's here, and whether I was exposed first or Ken was exposed first or we were both exposed simultaneously or at some other time, it's not important. That's just not the issue. That to me talks about our commitment. I don't want either of us to get sick, but I also don't know what I would do . . . if Ken got sick I would take care of him and vice versa—but I don't know if I want to be here when he's not. So that's gotten to be a much more real issue, as the years have passed. I don't think about it and dwell on it, but I just know that I would be incredibly unhappy if Ken—it's a real possibility; I try not to get bogged down with it. . . . Ken is totally into his work and gets very frustrated by it, and I'm worried that his frustration will impact his health. So that issue, of balancing professional life with personal health and well-being, is probably the most recurring issue that we have. HIV really pushed us together, but it also pushed us higher; it pushed us up to a different level of commitment to one another and to understanding of each other . . . the AIDS epidemic and the loss of our friends has, on the positive side, clarified life's priorities for us. I don't think I ever would have left the job I had, with a very good title, in a very dysfunctional company . . . but I felt like I needed to control things because it was important to me to spend more time with Ken and to be more in control of my time. So I made that decision. I think the same thing for Ken. The decision processes have become easier because we understand what's important. Our time-line is different and that's one of the things that has changed. Our time horizon was two months to six months. We had trouble making friends . . . but in the last five years we've progressed and pushed our time-line out; our vision of the horizon has moved up again. It's no longer watching our feet . . . we now look further ahead,

> and we now make plans for next summer, and for five years out, and we'll just keep doing it and take it as it comes. That's changed because of AIDS . . . taking things in the time we have more seriously and being able to discard those things which are not important. I used to care a lot more about what other people thought about me, and I don't care now . . . if it gives me pleasure or if it works for us, then that's fine, and that's what's important . . . on the expected time on the actuarial charts . . . we've broken the rules, and we've gotten away with it, and we've been very lucky. It may not always be that way.

Facing the spiritual pain associated with an infection that sooner or later will take life cannot be accepted and ultimately integrated into one's remaining days if genuine reconciliation does not happen. Keith was talking about the lack of blame for HIV that was possible because of the love in the relationship with Ken. He talked of what his partner meant to him and how difficult it would be to survive him. Keith identified a critical issue in adapting to their tragedy: the value of not dwelling on impending realities that one cannot control, namely, the time and circumstances of death. In a perverse way, HIV pushed Keith to think through what was important in his life and to make changes that probably would not have been made had he not become infected. He left a high-paying job to spend more time in the relationship with Ken. Facing the threat of death has its own way of doing one the favor of clarifying priorities about life and taking action to change at least some important realities.

Ken reflected on the significance of HIV on the relationship with Keith:

> I don't think it's really changed the relationship . . . the shift in the mid-eighties and what's important and what's not important and what we want to devote our energies to and what we want to let go by . . . that hasn't changed. We're continuing to live our lives seeing the significance of each day and not deferring for some future time things that would be good things for us to do today.

We will never know what happened to Keith and Ken, nor will they ever know of the significant contribution their story made to our research and our lives. Their voices talked of the resiliency of the human spirit, which finds its strength in loving relationships. Their words helped us understand how human beings found reasons for living when impending death, over which they had little control, loomed in the background. The gifts in a loving relationship enabled them to transcend the tragedy of HIV.

PSYCHOLOGICAL INTIMACY

Compared to physical intimacy, which included genital sex and bodily closeness such as touching and hugging, respondents talked of experiencing psychological intimacy when they were able to share their inner thoughts and feelings that were accepted, if not understood, by the partner. Such experiences were associated with feelings of connection, mutuality, and acceptance with one's partner. When respondents talked of being psychologically intimate with their partners, a sense of peace and contentment permeated their remarks. Those themes were evident as Daphne expressed what psychological intimacy meant to her:

> What has been good is the ongoing caring and respect and the sense that there is somebody there who really cares, who has your best interest, who loves you, who knows you better than anybody, and still likes you, and just that knowing, that familiarity, the depth of that knowing, the depth of that connection which is so incredibly meaningful. There is something spiritual after a while. It has a life of its own. This is what is really so comfortable.

Unlike sexual intimacy, which waned as couples grew older, psychological intimacy developed in a progressive direction. As sex became less satisfying and important to couples, words that suggested heightened levels of interpersonal connection, mutuality, and acceptance were used to describe relationships. Many respondents talked of how states of interpersonal closeness came to relationships after they and their partners had weathered difficult times. The pattern of psychological intimacy from early to recent years is shown in figure 6.2. There were differences in the patterns of psychological intimacy reported by gay and lesbian respondents. While less than 50 percent of gays described their relationships as psychologically intimate during the early years, more than 70 percent of lesbians described their relationships as psychologically intimate. During the middle years, the levels of psychological intimacy among lesbian couples regressed to levels characteristic of gay relationships, which remained constant from the early through the middle years. In recent years, the relationships of more than 70

Figure 6.2
Psychological Intimacy between Partners

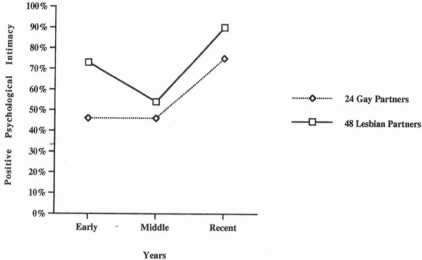

percent of all respondents were described as psychologically intimate. These patterns mirrored other developments in relationships, especially the increase in major conflict between lesbian partners during the middle years. Psychological intimacy was a casualty of serious interpersonal difficulties, which led to a disaffection and estrangement between partners. Until partners were able to find the means for resolving major conflict, which involved dealing openly with their feelings about their difficulties, psychological intimacy eluded them.

The differing relational orientations of men and women may have shaped patterns of intimacy. To experience intimacy, partners needed to focus their discussions on their relationships, that is, to process and reflect on their experiences together. A renewed sense of interpersonal connection, mutuality, and acceptance was one outcome of the process of reflecting on relational matters. Although most respondents described these kinds of experiences with their partners, lesbians were oriented more to relational processing than were gays.

Despite the observations that lesbian relationships are characterized by interpersonal fusion, the blurring of boundaries, and the resulting merger of two separate selves in a relationship, we found little evidence for such a hypothesis in this data. Rather, lesbian respondents talked of differentiation between them and their partners within a loving relationship. They valued separateness as significantly as they did connection within the context of relatedness with a partner. A lesbian couple spoke about those themes in their relationship. Initially, Isabelle commented on the relationship between physical affection and psychological intimacy:

> Physical affection has been fairly consistent across the time and probably has gotten more so because we've been able to be more emotionally intimate with each other . . . we've opened up, and communication has increased.

Isabelle then discussed the centrality of psychological intimacy in their relationship and her thoughts about the nature of fusion and differentiation:

> I don't get it when people say: "Oh, I could never talk about such and such with my partner because that would upset them, or I couldn't do this because they'd get so mad." I never had that. I feel like I can be who I am. Now, she doesn't always like everything about that. But I can still be that way, and I don't have to pretend. That's never been something that we've had to do. I would be horrified if that had to be. I just can't imagine what that's like. . . . I don't see us as fused. It's important to me not to be. I don't like it. I don't think it's healthy. It's one of those things where people can stay in relationships for years and years and years, from fifteen to seventy-five years, and that's how they do it, and they lose their individuality. I don't want to be in a relationship like that. It's important to me, for us, to be individuals as well.

Isabelle described what the relationship meant to her now:

> She's my best friend. Probably that's always been, but that means something different to me now. There's a peacefulness about that. We spend a lot of time together . . . if we're not together, I'm also happy . . . She's with me wherever I am. I can be whoever I am. I can say stuff to her that I would never say to anyone else. There are parts of myself that I don't particularly like, and I don't really share with other people, but it's OK to share with her. She'll take them in. She'll understand where it's coming from.

Ingrid spoke to her understanding of the interplay of connectedness and differentiation and how their interpersonal difficulties in the past made the quality of the connection more meaningful in recent years:

> Generally, we've gotten along very well. We like to be with each other. At the same time we've always had sort of different friends, but in the later part of our relationship we do have more mutual friends. . . . Although we like a lot of the same things, our interests are different. . . . I've appreciated the fact that she has been the one who will raise an issue or problem for the purpose of resolution, or improvement, and not just because she's angry or something. She seems to be willing to take that initiative. I didn't grow up in that kind of setting, so I think that's one reason this has worked. I think we both each really like the other one a lot. . . . There was a bond early on, in part because it was a different kind of relationship. . . . During the negative part, we were isolated for a long time, but that experience also bonded us. . . . I can be much more vulnerable. . . . I look to Isabelle for help with it, which wasn't something I knew how to do before.

Psychological intimacy between Isabelle and Ingrid represented how this quality developed in other relationships. Lesbian couples recalled high levels of intimacy early in relationships, only to have it decline during difficult times and then to return to even higher levels during recent years. Lesbian respondents described a delicate balance between the themes of connection and differentiation in their lives together. The strength of connection was important to the freedom of partners to be themselves, which meant that they pursued individual interests that often were not the same as their partners. These relationships seemed to offer them support to be themselves at home, in their social lives, and in their careers.

Compared to lesbians, several gays used language that suggested higher levels of fusion in their relationships. For example, Barry thought he and his partner had become "more and more dependent on each other . . . it's more and more a meshing of two spirits." Commonly the theme of fusion was balanced by observations of differentiation within connectedness, not unlike lesbian relationships. Daniel and Dwight spoke of the integration of these qualities in their relationship. Daniel said that friends had made the observation that he and Dwight "tend to do everything together." He went on to say:

> We really enjoy each other, and it's rare that we do things separately, but I think it's good to do things separately, and on occasion we certainly do, but for us we don't find great need to do a lot separately. A lot of friends don't understand that . . . as if it were something negative . . . at this point in my life, I feel that

the love for him and my desire to be with him is much more important than anything else.

The importance of connection to Dwight was evident as Daniel talked. While acknowledging that quality as an attribute, he made the observation that others may not have understood the nature of their relationship. Dwight emphasized interpersonal differentiation as he discussed the relationship. He remembered the difficulties of the early years when the level of psychological intimacy between them was at its lowest point. After many of the tensions between them were worked through during the middle years, Dwight thought that:

> Emotionally, things are really good now . . . it feels good knowing I'm growing old with Daniel even though we're very different people, in that I'm very social, and I have a lot of friends, and he's not as social, and he doesn't have as many friends. . . . I mean it's not exclusively that way. But much more lopsided. . . . We both place a really great importance on togetherness. We make sure that we have dinner together every night, and we have our weekend activities that we make sure we do together. . . . It's very important. But I think that both of us understand it's also important to be an individual and have your own life. . . . I think you become really uninteresting to each other if you don't have another life you can come back and share. . . . You need to bring things into the relationship . . . that keep it growing and changing.

Dwight's comments represented how most partners viewed the mixture of connectedness with fusion as they discussed psychological intimacy. When one partner identified a specific personal characteristic, as was evident in the interviews with Daniel and Dwight, the other partner often identified a differing characteristic. Although these complementary differences stimulated conflict, they also had the function of enriching relationships and helping individuals find a sense of wholeness in their lives. Partners found intimacy not only in their similarities, which nurtured merger, but in the differences that brought vitality into relationships.

SUMMARY

Intimacy as a sense of communion between partners was experienced in the sexual, physical, and psychological dimensions of relationships. Sexual intimacy, very important early in relationships, began to wane after several years. As the frequency and satisfaction with genital sex declined, psychological intimacy developed among most respondents. Hugging, touching, and physical closeness remained relatively constant throughout the years in contrast to the regression in sexual intimacy and the progression in psychological intimacy. Despite the change in sexual intimacy, genital sex continued to be seen as important from early through recent years.

The advent of HIV has had an enormous impact on sexual relations of both homosexuals and heterosexuals. In addition to changing sexual behaviors, particularly in the direction of making people aware of the dangers of engaging in unprotected genital sex, this lethal virus has stimulated a reappraisal of many aspects of relationships. The story of two male partners, who were both infected with HIV ten years before this study, was changed profoundly by the intrusion of that virus into their lives. The responses of these two men speak to the quality of their lives as they realize increasingly that their horizon gets closer and closer each day. Their voices were an inspiration to the adaptive capacities of human beings in how they transcended tragedy and did not allow despair to rule their lives.

As the couples in this study grew older together, the experience of psychological intimacy was marked by a deepening sense of relational communion between them. Self-awareness along with openness to one's partner became a reality as acceptance and understanding were integrated into their relationships. Intimacy involved the interplay of two dynamics, fusion and differentiation. A sense of oneness needed to be part of relationships for couples to experience a sense of psychological intimacy. Differences brought balance to relationships, which enabled individuals to experience a sense of wholeness within the connection to the partner.

Within these relationships, we found little evidence for the hypothesis that lesbian partners are connected through fusion. Rather, a sense of oneness was complemented by differences that enabled partners to be psychologically intimate while maintaining their individuality. A similar theme was evident in the voices of gays as they spoke about psychological intimacy. Although several gay partners spoke of fusion, they, too, talked of the importance of differences in providing liveliness and balance within their relationships.

7

Social Supports

Our friends get to know us for who we are . . . that's supportive.

While mutual support between partners nourished self-esteem and contributed significantly to relational stability, acceptance and help from others was important to individuals and couples. First, we explored how respondents perceived their families and the families of their partners as sources of support. They were asked how parents, brothers, and sisters reacted upon hearing of their sexual orientations and their relationships with partners. We also explored the significance of the reactions of family members to their relationships over the years. A second potential source of social support was religion, so we inquired about its significance to their relationships. As 68 percent of respondents had been in psychotherapy, which was usually focused on relational issues with partners, we asked them to talk about the effects of therapy on relationships, a third source of support. A fourth area of inquiry were the friends of respondents, which included their involvement in gay and lesbian organizations.

FAMILIES

The reactions of families to the "news" about the sexual orientation of respondents and their relationships with partners were complex. Coming out as a lesbian or gay couple was generally the first open acknowledgment to the family of one's sexual orientation. Openness about these relationships often confirmed the sexual orientation of a son or daughter, a brother or sister.

Families varied in their initial reactions to the "news." Overall, the families of gays were more supportive than were those of lesbians. Only 15 percent of lesbian respondents compared with 42 percent of gays described their families as supportive upon first hearing of the relationships with partners. Respondents viewed the families of their partners as somewhat more supportive; 31 percent of lesbians and 50 percent of gays considered their partners' families supportive. Over the years, the responses of families became more supportive; 50 percent of gays and 40 percent of lesbians described their families as supportive in recent years.

Family responses varied from overt rejection to acceptance. Acceptance generally reflected the supportive styles that had characterized family relations, even when individual reactions of family members varied. Sarah described such a response:

> My parents are generally warm and open toward people, so that was their general demeanor toward Samantha and me. They met her before they knew we were involved. . . . I would say on a scale of most people's parents, they had a pretty easy time. There were some things that were harder for my mother; she worried a lot about our decision to have children. They clearly both accept our family and accept Samantha as my partner. . . . My dad didn't have particular problems at all with accepting it; there were some times when it was difficult for my mother, but overall she fully accepts it. My brothers have always fully accepted it. . . . I worried about my grandmother, but after she came to visit us one time, she sent us a card with two little birds on the cover that said: "Thank you two love birds for showing me such a good time." That let us know.

The reactions of some families were not as predictable as they were in Sarah's family. A liberal set of values did not necessarily mean that the "news" of one's sexual orientation and relationship with a same-sex partner would be accepted. In the relationship of Daniel and Dwight, family reactions were the opposite of what each partner had anticipated. Daniel described their parents' responses:

> Initially, it was a little different for Dwight's parents because they found out he was gay and living with a man at the same time. It surprised me that his parents reacted more negative and more hostile than my parents. My parents were not educated. My father didn't finish high school, and my mother was a farm girl . . . they were very conservative, but they were much more understanding. . . . Dwight's parents are more educated . . . they're liberals. I think that it's great to intellectually say: "I accept gay people," but when it comes down to being your son, then you lose it . . . his mother hung up the phone and didn't talk to him for six months. His father even suggested psychiatric treatment. So it was a very stressful, negative period.

Although parents may have been overtly rejecting when they heard of a son's or daughter's sexual orientation and relationship, as were the parents of Dwight, other family members responded differently. Daniel continued:

> We got a lot of support from Dwight's sisters when they found out. He told his mother first, before he told his sisters, even though they had known and were waiting for him to open up . . . after the fact they were like: "Well, why didn't you come to us first because we could have helped you."

The theme of sibling support was reported commonly among families in which parents reacted in a rejecting way. Sometimes entire families were allied against their offspring, but it was more common for reactions to vary between members as in Dwight's family. If siblings had positive relationships with parents, they were instrumental in bringing about parental acceptance. The process of change in the attitudes of parents toward a couple was described by Daniel:

> Dwight's sisters were always very supportive to his parents. So I think his parents grew to understand better because of their input and their feelings about me and our relationship.

The patience of partners and their persistence in reaching out to parents in an accepting manner also helped modify negative responses. That modification occurred not only as a result of the influence of siblings and the manner of partners but also because some partners shared interests with parents that brought them together. Daniel commented on the relationship in recent years with Dwight's mother:

> His mother and I are now very close; we share books and talk. I treat her like I treat my mother, and I think she respects that.

Among many parents who struggled over the years to accept the reality of their child's sexual orientation and same-sex relationship, the residuals of homophobic attitudes became visible from time to time. Although the intervention of siblings and the patience of partners helped to move relations with parents in a positive direction, negative feelings were sometimes hidden or obscured by overt gestures of reconciliation. Roberta talked of her mother's struggle to reconcile with her and to establish a positive relationship with both partners:

> On a gift-giving occasion like Christmas, my mother sent this great wool blanket, and the next year she also sent something else that was bed related. It was really significant. Like, suddenly how she interacted with me and Regina changed after those two gifts. Something about her coming to grips with my relationship was marked by sending me stuff that was for our bed. I know that she processed a lot of it with a group of women. . . . Now she is fine . . . she and Regina talk regularly, sometimes more regularly than I do.

Gifts symbolic of the nature of the relationships between partners were one means of marking a shift toward parental support. Parents who overtly communicated their acceptance and support of relationships frequently kept their conflicted feelings hidden. Sometimes those feelings emerged on specific occasions. For example, some respondents talked of how the birthdays of their partners were ignored in families that customarily acknowledged such occasions; others described partners not being "remembered" with a gift at Christmas. Roberta discussed how the residuals of hidden feelings would be expressed by her mother:

> She has some problems understanding some things. Shortly after our first child was born, I was talking to her about how hard it was to deal with day care and work. She just said: "all the single parents I know say that." It was like: "mom, I am not a single parent, remember? There is another parent!" Then, when we

decided to adopt a kid, I was telling mom about that: "we are going to adopt another kid." She said: "oh, that's cool! Will I be this kid's grandmother?" . . . she had to ask that question.

Several lesbians commented on the reactions of their mothers, which suggested a triangular dynamic among mothers, daughters, and partners. Dana described how jealous her mother was of Diane during the early years of their relationship. The mother and daughter had been accustomed to spending much time together until Dana met Diane. In fact, both Dana and Diane described their mothers as similar and how crowded the psychological scene became whenever they visited with either family:

Her mother was a little jealous of us at the beginning. Dana had been and still is a very close daughter to her mother. They have a very good relationship. But her mother couldn't understand why, all of a sudden, she wanted to be with somebody like me. In the beginning my mother was probably jealous like Dana's mother. My mother would say: "when your friend is here, I can't talk to you." . . . When Dana was around, my mother would say: "She sat here the whole time and I wanted to talk to you," and I would say: "Ma, you can say anything you want in front of Dana," and she would say: "Oh, no. You can't talk about family things." . . . When I finally got the guts to tell her about us, my mother started crying. . . . I'm hugging her and telling her not to cry, that it is OK and I'm very happy. And she said: "Diane, who is the man and who is the woman?" And I said: "nobody is the man and nobody is the woman. We are two women."

While a majority of families experienced considerable difficulty in accepting and being supportive of their adult children's sexual orientation and relationships, there was less acceptance among the families of lesbians than among gays. The responses of mothers to lesbian daughters were different from the responses of fathers who often seemed to blend into the background. Compared to parents, siblings generally reacted with more support, and their acceptance was a vehicle for gradual modifications in parental attitudes. Among lesbians who became parents, their children were a vehicle for modifying negative parental attitudes. Of great importance was the gradual change in attitudes that occurred in parents and other family members as their relationships with both partners developed. That process usually took several years before partners, who may have been "blamed" for the unacceptable lifestyle of a family's adult child, were viewed as human beings rather than as objects shaped by guilt and homophobic stereotypes. As parents and others could "see" over time that these relationships were happy, their guilt was abated, and they were able to replace rejection with acceptance.

RELIGION

Involvement in organized religious practices played a marginal role in the lives of gays and lesbians. During the early years, 56 percent of all respondents said that religion had no influence on their lives or on their relationships with partners; two out of ten gays and three out of ten lesbians reported religion as a positive force in their lives. In recent years, religion had a more influential effect on lesbians; one-half of lesbians viewed religion as a positive force in their lives. The significance of religion to gay respondents did not change appreciably from early to recent years.

Membership with a partner in a religious organization or group was very supportive to a minority of respondents; those respondents referred to the "commonality" of values they shared with their partners. More often than not, these groups, such as Reformed Judaism and Quakerism, were identified with a significant social justice mission. Sometimes individuals met their future partners through involvement in the same synagogue, church, or meeting house. The commonality of values was not only a basis for bringing partners together but for supporting the bond between them throughout the years.

Even though most respondents were indifferent to religious practices and beliefs, the history of involvement in organized religion in childhood continued to influence their lives. Several respondents carried within them bitter memories of their experiences with religious figures, especially Catholic priests and Protestant ministers; many remembered being rebuked and reprimanded for their sexual orientations. Nancy spoke of the "pervasive influence" of her religious background on her life as an adult:

> I think there are two parts to how religion played a part in our relationship. . . . One is the continuing effects of my very traditional, Catholic upbringing. I went to Catholic school until I went to college . . . so I have a very fundamental identity as a rule- and ritual-based Catholic. I continue to look for rules and rituals in life. That is part of me, whether I acknowledge it or not,

which is totally different from Nina . . . she was brought up in the Unitarian Church. There just wasn't the same kind of dogma. She tries really hard to make allowances for that component of my being, but she doesn't get how pervasive that influence is for me. That is part of my insistence on sexual monogamy. It has probably influenced our relationship but mostly in ways we probably can't really identify. For me because it is too close, and for her because it is too foreign.

Nancy spoke about an important theme, which, as she said, may not have been within consciousness all the time. The memories of bad experiences, such as being ridiculed or condemned for their homosexuality, tended to be at the forefront of consciousness and often obscured other memories. For many respondents, past experiences led to the rejection of religion, but for others it sparked a continual yearning for meaning in their lives and a search for "spirituality." Nancy talked about her search:

I feel the need to have some sort of spiritual dimension in life. . . . I have searched and have not found any traditional place where we can be fully accepted. I would go back to Catholicism in a minute just for the ritual, because I found it so comforting. But I can't even find one point of agreement in what the Church is offering, so I can't do it and can't take my kids there. We have looked at traditional Christian churches, all of which are fairly alienating. We have looked at Judaism, which is close but not really a cigar. The thing about being a Buddhist is that it is so individualistic; it doesn't fulfill my need for group ritual, which I think takes you out of your everyday experience and makes it so much broader. I can't find it. We do try to maintain the possibility of a spiritual life. We talk about it a lot.

The search for spiritual meaning in life of which Nancy spoke was expressed by several respondents, mostly among lesbians during recent years. Despite feelings that religious institutions had "no room" for them, many individuals and couples spoke of a need to connect again with their roots. Octavia and Olivia described their spiritual heritage as Jews and their quest to connect with that part of their identity in recent years. Octavia said:

Olivia and I are both Jewish, and we were both fairly disconnected from that when we got together, although, at some gut level, I think it was important to us in terms of similar ethnic backgrounds. But in terms of the religious component, that really didn't become important to us until somehow we found our way back through a gay Jewish group. . . . I was raised as an Orthodox Jew and certainly, in that venue, there was no room for my lifestyle as a lesbian. Olivia was raised in a conservative temple but not really participating, so where I had a lot of background, she didn't have very much. We had both given it up . . . we both kind of realized that spirituality was important and also a connection. It's kind of hard to separate the religious from the ethnic when you are Jewish. The connection to our roots was very important, so we got more and more involved.

Octavia described their search for involvement with a religious group. The availability of groups that were exploring spirituality did not "speak" to their needs to integrate their identity as a lesbian couple with the cultural and religious heritage they shared. Octavia described their experiences:

Maybe we really had to have the spirituality come through in a Jewish setting . . . that affected our relationship in that we could be in a relationship that was recognized at least by this gay Jewish group. We haven't ever gone through any ceremonies or anything like that, but it was important. We both grew into it at the same time when our first child was born . . . it was actually very beautiful, we created a ritual naming ceremony for him in this group. We had all of our friends. It was very Jewish, and it was very gay identified, and it was who we were as a family.

She went on to identify another important link between the need to connect with their joint heritage as Jews and their decision to become parents:

Although we were connected to this group before we had kids, somehow having kids made you think about what is my religious identity and what do I want for my kids? . . . and a need to pass on some of the ethical lessons that I want to pass on. Soon after becoming parents, we joined a temple . . . that continues to do a lot of outreach to the gay and lesbian community and has a lot of gay and lesbian people as part of their larger community. . . . They also have a lot of lesbians with kids now. This is a place where you can be comfortable being who you are, and you want to keep going there; it has been very important to us.

According to Olivia, religion had become progressively more important in their relationship since the birth of their first child. Despite their
similar religious and ethnic backgrounds, the strength of their values
was different. Octavia was raised in an orthodox Jewish family and
Olivia by a Jewish mother and a non-Jewish father, both of whom were
quite liberal about religious practices. Olivia attended a conservative
temple but was much less religiously observant than Octavia. She felt
that connection with Judaism "was important to us but not in the
religious sense . . . it became more important when kids came." Both
partners felt that identification with their religious and cultural heritage
through membership in a temple was an important part of their lives
and a significant source of support in their relationship.

Respondents who considered religion a source of support, as Octavia
and Olivia did, were likely to be Jews rather than Christians. Even when
Jewish congregations were not hospitable because of their relationships, rabbis were often described as welcoming.

PSYCHOTHERAPY

Therapy was an important source of support to the relationships of
almost seven out of ten respondents who had been in some type of
psychotherapy since committing to their partners. Eighty-three percent
of lesbians compared to 38 percent of gays had been involved in either
individual or couples psychotherapy. The most common mode of
therapy reported by 47 percent of all respondents was couples psychotherapy in which both partners were treated together by the same
therapist. Of the seventeen couples in that mode of therapy, sixteen
were lesbians; only one gay couple reported psychotherapy as a couple.
Couples therapy focused on relationships, particularly communication
difficulties.

The following couple discussed what led them to seek psychotherapy.
Isabelle remembered the early years of their relationship as a time when
they "argued less and probably communicated less," yet "we got along
fine," which she attributed to compatibility in their lifestyles. Avoidance
of conflict, associated with unspoken differences between them, led to
feelings of estrangement and unhappiness with the relationship. Ingrid
described how she experienced life with Isabelle and how therapy
enabled them to modify ingrained patterns of avoidance:

In retrospect, we probably didn't communicate very well . . . not knowing what to do with anger. . . . I came from a family that didn't communicate that much, and . . . Isabelle came from a very verbal family. I don't think I necessarily recognized that until she pointed it out. . . . In the beginning, we didn't communicate well about things we were angry about or disappointed in. I was used to holding that stuff in . . . we probably got over humps by not dealing with it and sort of just getting on with it. When we went to couples therapy, that's really the first time I think that we had looked at how we were communicating or not, and learned some tools about how to talk about things, particularly difficult things; that was helpful. . . . Isabelle is the more verbal one . . . if we get angry at each other about something, she'll tend to be very verbal about it, and I'll tend to shut up. Sometimes I feel barraged by all this verbalness that I just shut up. So that's a dynamic that neither of us is really happy with. But we definitely are aware of it and try to address it when it's happening.

Despite her assertiveness in the relationship, Isabelle was conflicted about coming out socially, which she thought contributed to the tensions in the relationship. Her partner's silence about their relational difficulties seemed to be a reminder of her public silence about her sexual identity. Isabelle commented on the connection between these two aspects of her life:

Couples counseling was the start to help us feel more OK. It was part of our coming out process and to be more self-accepting. . . . When you can do that, when that moves along, it's easy to talk. It was helping us to move along a little bit and be able to talk about what was going on. We didn't make great strides, but it really did start the whole thing. We went to our first gay pride parade. Then of course women's music. We were coming out to a lot more people.

Each partner was troubled by somewhat differing concerns that had negative effects on their relationship. As they began to focus in the therapy on their differences, Isabelle talked of the struggle to modify behaviors. Their persistence in that difficult process resulted in better feelings about themselves and the relationship:

There was lots that we did talk about, but in terms of our relationship, we each had a life that we didn't share with each

> other. We really had to learn that it was important to talk about this stuff. Neither of us has a tolerance for lengthy talk to move from one place to another; we can stop now and then come back to it. Oftentimes that's just hearing the other person and then trying to get clear about saying what it is we want to say. We can do it! We do it pretty successfully . . . it's not the easiest part; I think some people have an easier time of it . . . early on, when we weren't really talking as much, there was not as much negotiation.

The theme of finding ways of communicating about differences and negotiating modifications in behaviors was identified as respondents talked about the value of therapy to their relationships. As with Isabelle and Ingrid, couples therapy was viewed as a process that supported modifications in behaviors that had prevented partners from reaching higher adaptive plateaus in their personal and relational development. These two dimensions were interrelated, so that modifications began either within a partner or in their styles of communicating as a couple. Psychotherapy served as a catalyst to initiate the process of behavioral modification.

Despite their differences, which were attributed to family backgrounds, Ingrid thought their "basic patterns" of dealing with feelings about differences were "the same." Similar to other couples, Isabelle and Ingrid used therapy to identify and understand what had been perceived as different ways of dealing with conflict between them. As partners explored in therapy how they were different, they discovered they had more in common than was apparent to them. Ingrid commented on the similarities in their underlying anxieties and fears:

> The basic patterns are the same . . . we each express anger more easily than we ever did . . . overall, I think she's always understood me pretty well. The area that I feel the least understood may not have changed a whole lot . . . it's when we're in conflict, and she wants me to talk more than I want to talk and gets angry at me that I don't do that. I can feel misunderstood then . . . that's still an area where I feel sort of alone. . . . When I get asked to do something that at the moment I don't think I can do or won't do for whatever reason . . . I don't think either of us came into this relationship being great communicators or problem solvers. . . . For me a big change was that I learned all about sharing . . . that's second nature now.

The overt behaviors of these partners "looked" quite different to them. Isabelle became assertive when she experienced anxiety associated with relational conflict; as Isabelle became increasingly assertive, Ingrid withdrew. As therapy enabled each partner to explore these differences, they began to "see" the similarities in their underlying anxieties and fears. For them and other partners, learning about oneself and acquiring interpersonal skills to communicate effectively with partners was the most common gain from couples psychotherapy. According to respondents, therapy offered partners new relational skills that were used to negotiate differences between them. Effective communication based on listening, acceptance, and understanding helped to neutralize anger and guilt that had previously undermined relationships.

Not all experiences with therapy worked out as well as with Isabelle and Ingrid. Partners often "shopped" for a therapist until they found a "good enough fit" with their needs and goals. Not infrequently the fit included the sexual orientation of therapists but not always. Several respondents said they had been treated successfully by heterosexual therapists. Qualities of caring, empathy, and technical competence were identified as more important than the sexual orientation of a therapist.

Even when there were problems in the match between a therapist and a couple, therapy sometimes was instrumental in starting the process of behavioral modification. Similar to Isabelle and Ingrid, Daniel reported that the relationship with Dwight seemed to be "working" during the early years. According to Daniel, they took the relationship for granted and focused on their careers rather than on the communication difficulties between them:

> We started making assumptions about what the other person was thinking, what the other person wanted, and which ended up leading to problems. We recognized that we were not communicating . . . we were just going along and not listening to each other the way we had done before. So we decided to go to counseling . . . the counseling really didn't work for us; we went three or four months to a gay man, but we recognized that we needed to communicate; the sessions were good because we allotted this time together once a week, so we talked about trying to do this on our own . . . you know, a couple of hours a week or a half an hour in the evening, we would talk about things, the way you make me feel . . . we hadn't done that before.

Daniel went on to discuss how their experience in doing therapy by themselves challenged their customary styles of relating:

> It's an ongoing struggle to continue to talk and to be honest . . . to not make assumptions about what the other person is thinking . . . to not assume what Dwight's going to end up saying when he begins to talk . . . to not complete sentences for him. That's for anybody, in any relationship. . . . It's hard . . . just recognizing each other and not taking things for granted.

In talking about their efforts to help themselves, Dwight said that he and Daniel "realized" that:

> You have to make yourself communicate. It's not always something that comes naturally. We don't fight that much now. We bicker, but we don't fight. . . . There are things which we do together which are designed to help us communicate. We have dinner together every night, and the TV's off, and we sit at the dining room table, and we talk. . . . On weekends we have schedules and do things together. Having the ritual of dinner and the ritual of what we do on the weekends is very helpful in helping us communicate . . . now we're very direct with each other. We're very honest . . . when we're mad we say we're mad . . . neither one of us really hold a lot back. So I'd say the quality is pretty good.

The most prevalent theme in the comments of respondents about psychotherapy was its catalytic effect on modifying relational behaviors. Ingrained styles of communication often compromised a need for psychological intimacy, which became increasingly important as the years passed. Therapy was a social support that enabled couples to modify their roles as they learned new ways of communicating their needs and expectations.

FRIENDS

Friends were important to most respondents. Perhaps because of the lack of support by many families and religious groups, friendships became a primary support system for most couples. As Ian, who has been with his partner for twenty-six years, observed, "friends become family; we celebrate Christmas with one group, New Year's with another group, and Easter with a third group." For the few respondents who had no friends, they felt that the relationships with their partners were sufficient to meet their needs and that other relationships might threaten their partnership. For example, after acknowledging that support from friends might "enrich" the relationship with his partner, Brian commented, "it is certainly not fatal if we do not have friends . . . they might be supportive, but they might also be destructive." His partner, Barry, felt that avoiding friendships kept the relationship "safe."

Having friends and considering them a part of one's support system depended on the historical experiences and patterns of needing and making friends. Gary and George had a small circle of friends who had been loyal to them for years. Gary reported that "we have a very active role with friends and family . . . especially friends." George's experience with friends was reported quite differently:

> I don't surround myself with a lot of people, I really don't. I've learned, unfortunately, not to confide in my family, I can't define them as a support system. I have one intimate, one person that I kind of confide in, but I don't really have a lot of people around me. I never really thought of this, but in my whole life, I've never surrounded myself with people; I take care of myself.

Even when couples were surrounded by mutual friends, these friendships may have had a different significance to each partner as the comments of Gary and George illustrated. Grace also spoke of how she "was totally immersed in a lot of primary relationships . . . we had a lot of differences in that way. She had a couple of friends and a lot of political acquaintances and work people, but not a lot of close friends." In general, partners shared friends, even though several partners said they maintained separate relationships outside their circle of mutual friends. Often these individual friendships were made at work or had been established before partners formed their committed relationships, as was the case with Grace and Gwen.

Regarding the sexual orientation of friends, lesbians talked differently than gays. Although a lesbian partner might maintain a friendship with a heterosexual woman with whom she worked, the close friendships of lesbians were usually with other lesbians. These friendships were almost always mutual ones. Florence and Felicia spoke of the importance of same-sex friendships. Florence said:

> For both of us, what family is now are our lesbian friends.

Felicia also valued lesbian friendships that were very meaningful to their relationship:

> I can't imagine being a couple without friends. It would be like being castaways on an island.

Compared to lesbians, gays talked of friendships with both homosexual and heterosexual couples. Many gay respondents spoke of the difficulty in meeting and making friends with other gay couples. Dwight spoke about that theme:

> Friends have been very supportive . . . actually most of them are heterosexuals. It's supportive that they treat us like anybody else . . . there's a real need to feel acceptance from other people . . . you have the sense of being alone particularly in the whole coming out process. . . . We don't know very many gay couples like us. A lot of our couple friends are straight. That's a problem in the gay culture. You're not supported as a couple. The gay clubs are for singles, for meeting and for having sex. They overlook couples. We'd love to socialize with couples like us, but there's no channel for finding them. . . . We are able to get together with straight friends and talk about anything that friends talk about. We don't get singled out because we are a gay couple. Our friends value us for who we are. That's supportive!

Friendships were affirming of one's sexual orientation and helped to neutralize the social isolation that was a threat in the lives of these couples. Friends offered acceptance to partners as human beings who happened to have a same-sex orientation. To gay partners, acceptance enabled them to experience a sense of validation about their relationships.

Even when individual partners had their own friends, couples experienced isolation, especially if they were closeted. Ingrid discussed that dilemma:

> In the early years . . . probably one of the things that wasn't so good was we were fairly isolated. That was more of a period when we each had friends outside of the relationship; we weren't necessarily out to those people . . . in the last five or six years our ability to make relationships that both of us have with other lesbian couples has been very reinforcing . . . to have that support.

The link between being closeted and the development of mutual friendships was evident in the observations of Ingrid. It was not unusual for partners to have individual friends early in relationships, when partners may not have been open socially about their sexual orientation. Shared friendships developed as each partner became ready to acknowledge her sexual identity. That development may have been related to the changing social context in which gay and lesbian organizations have been supportive in affirming homosexual lifestyles and same-sex relationships.

Friendships were also supportive in taking pressure off relationships. It was stressful for partners to rely on one another as their only source of support. Ingrid talked of friendships in that way:

> Isabelle's not always there for me the way I want, but that's not realistic. That's why we have other friends . . . so that the whole burden of being there isn't just on one person. At least that's the way I feel, because that's pretty tough. . . . We have mostly lesbian, some gay friends . . . other people are very important to us. Experiencing ourselves as a couple, I think, is important. When you relate to other people and friends, they experience you as a couple; you experience them as a couple. I think that's important. It's validating. It's just kind of life. It's what people do. It's normalizing. It's what straight people do.

Friendships offered individual partners and couples support in several ways. Friends neutralized the potential for social isolation by helping individuals accept their sexual orientations and by acknowledging the validity of their relationships. An important challenge to adaptation in these relationships was in negotiating mutual friendships, particularly when individuals had different needs for friends. Lesbians developed mutual friends with other lesbian couples over the years, a pattern different from gays who had more friendships with heterosexuals. Friendships were also supportive in enabling individuals to come out about themselves and their relationships. Finally, individuals relied on friends in times of stress when partners were not available, which took pressure off relationships.

SUMMARY

The meaning of support from family, religion, therapy, and friends was explored in this chapter. Of these four potential sources of social support, family and religion were viewed as the least supportive. A minority of families responded in an accepting way to the "news" that their adult son or daughter was a homosexual. Coming out as a gay or lesbian couple was usually the first explicit acknowledgment to a family of one's sexual orientation. Although parents were more rejecting than siblings on finding out about the sexual orientation and relationships of partners, there was considerable modification in attitudes toward acceptance over the years. Brothers and sisters who were initially supportive were often a valuable resource in the rapprochement with parents. In recent years, fewer than one-half of families were accepting of these partners and their relationships. Even when families were seen as supportive, several of them manifested considerable ambivalence in accepting these relationships, such as forgetting the birthdays of partners or not including them in holiday celebrations.

Involvement in religious practices played a marginal role in the lives of a majority of respondents, although more lesbians than gays became involved in religious experiences in recent years. That involvement was frequently with groups that had a spiritual mission rather than with traditional religious institutions. Often the indifference or negative response to traditional churches was connected to past experiences with clergy. Jewish respondents had more favorable experience with Judaism than Catholics or Protestants and were more likely to be active in religious practices. Rabbis seemed to have responded with greater acceptance than priests and ministers.

For almost seven out of ten respondents, psychotherapy served as an important source of support. Significantly more lesbians than gays were involved in therapy, which focused generally on enhancing relationships through resolving communication difficulties. Therapy was depicted as a resource that stimulated partners to examine their relationships and as a vehicle for learning new skills for enhancing communication.

Most respondents valued friendships that were experienced, next to their relationships, as the most important source of individual and couple support. The few respondents who did not feel a need for friendships reported a lifelong pattern of not having friends and felt that the relationships with partners offered enough support; a few of these respondents expressed the fear that making "friends" could threaten the stability of relationships. For most respondents, friends served as extended families, which was important given the lack of acceptance and support from their families. Although many friendships began in relationships with individual partners, couple friendships became more common in recent years. Often the process of developing joint friends was associated with partners coming out and feeling confident about being identified as a same-sex couple. Lesbian friendships were almost always with other lesbians, while gay friendships just as often were with heterosexual couples. More than lesbians, gays talked about the difficulties of finding and making friends with other gay couples, as gay social life catered to singles. Friendships were valued for acceptance, understanding, and validation of relationships; friends also helped to take the pressure off relationships during difficult times.

8

Relationships Are Relationships

It's too bad that people, when they talk about homosexuals, just think about the sex act, when it's really a relationship . . . it's the caring, the feeling, the understanding that we have for one another.

The title of this final chapter and the quotation above speak to the heart of our findings. Because the data upon which this book was based were part of our research on adult relationships that last (Mackey and O'Brien 1995), we had the unusual opportunity to compare same-sex and heterosexual relationships. This chapter explores heterosexual and same-sex data about roles, relational fit, conflict including its management, decision making, and sexual and psychological intimacy.

The instrument of data collection was essentially the same for all our studies. While the time frames for our studies of heterosexual and same-sex couples were somewhat different, they were similar enough for developing an understanding of how committed relationships evolved over the years. That data permitted us to get a glimpse of the similarities and differences in these relationships during early, middle, and recent years.

Although we were reasonably successful in matching heterosexual couples with same-sex couples by educational level and religious backgrounds, there were significant differences between the two groups in the following characteristics: age, years together, and the parameters of the early, middle, and recent years. Heterosexual respondents were older than gay and lesbian respondents. Approximately 50 percent of gays and lesbians and 13 percent of heterosexuals were under fifty years of age; 24 percent of gays and lesbians were over sixty years of age compared to 46 percent of heterosexual respondents. All same-sex couples had been together more than fifteen years but less than thirty years, with the exception of one gay couple that had been together more than thirty years; 67 percent of same-sex couples had been together between fifteen and twenty years. Sixty-seven percent of heterosexual couples had been together more than thirty years.

All heterosexual couples had children. The early years for that group were defined as the years before the birth of the first child; the middle years were synonymous with child rearing, which began with the birth of the oldest child; the recent years were the post-parenting or empty nest years, which began with the youngest child's eighteenth birthday. These periods had floating time boundaries. This was somewhat different from the same-sex couples in which the early years covered approximately the first five years together, the middle years the next five years, and the recent years those years after being together for ten years. These time markers were not imposed rigidly on same-sex respondents but used as flexible tags to bring consistency to our explorations and to the analysis of data. In fact, the boundaries that defined the early, middle, and recent years for same-sex couples were quite fluid and frequently extended below or beyond these markers; among heterosexual couples, markers varied depending on the time of the births of the oldest and youngest children.

Research on commitment between partners in heterosexual and same-sex relationships has focused on twin factors: the strength of attraction between partners and the barriers against ending relationships (Peplau 1991). Among the respondents in our studies, commitment meant an affirmation of loyalty to a partner regardless of the sexual orientation of the couple. For many gay and lesbian couples, commitment was framed as a pledge to remain in the relationship as long as it was a positive resource in the psychological, social, and spiritual development of each partner. Among heterosexual couples, personal commitment was reinforced by the legal and religious bond between them, although they rarely thought of divorce as an option for resolving marital difficulties. There are numerous rights, privileges, as well as responsibilities that are part of marriage which same-sex couples do not have. Winfeld (1996) estimated that "there are 170-plus rights and responsibilities that go with legal marriage." Same-sex couples are either denied or must take unusual steps to own property jointly, to inherit property of the partner, to receive the pension and Social Security benefits of a deceased partner, and to be protected by privacy rights enjoyed by those legally married.

In the following discussion we explore the significance of various patterns of relationships. The goal is to understand how different dimensions of relationships unfolded as heterosexual and same-sex partners lived out their lives together.

ROLES: SAME-SEX AND HETEROSEXUAL RELATIONSHIPS

Roles in the relationships of heterosexual and same-sex couples were structured very differently. Among heterosexual respondents, roles were described in traditional ways. Almost without exception, men expected to work and provide for their families, and women expected to stay at home to become mothers and to care for their families. These traditional expectations carried over to role behaviors in marriage and resulted in a differentiation of tasks and responsibilities throughout the early years and into the child-rearing years. By that time, husbands were responsive to sharing parenting roles, and the differences between spouses, at least in this dimension of their relationships, became less differentiated by sex. All same-sex partners had nontraditional expectations about relational roles. Sharing responsibilities for the household, mutuality in making decisions that affected their relationships, and flexibility in negotiating tasks, such as cooking, were usually decided according to one's talents and skills. The roles of heterosexual couples mirrored the prevailing cultural norms about gender roles in marriage that characterized the 1950s and 1960s when most of these couples married. There were no prevailing cultural norms that had an influential effect on shaping relational roles of same-sex couples. As a consequence, they had to work out roles as they moved through the early years of their relationships.

Despite the differences between same-sex and heterosexual partners in their roles, there were similarities in their "choices" of role models with whom they identified in order to structure their relationships. Parents were the most commonly reported role models for all respondents. However, gays and lesbians compared to heterosexuals were more likely to identify with at least one parent as their primary role models. Almost 80 percent of lesbians, 60 percent of gays, and 50 percent of heterosexuals reported that their role behaviors were similar to at least one parent. Frequently mentioned similarities were a caring attitude toward one's partner, respect of a parent for the spouse, love, support, and commitment to the relationship. Clearly these characteristics came, in part, from identifications with admired qualities in a parent, which were incorporated into an individual's sense of self in relationships with partners.

The lower percent of heterosexual respondents who identified with at least one parent as a role model may have been related to the ages and "generation gap" between them. That is, heterosexuals were more likely to have parents whom they perceived as different from them in educational levels, socioeconomic status, and lifestyles. It was not unusual for heterosexuals to have come from families in which their parents were first generation citizens who were poor and struggling to assimilate into the mainstream. Among homosexual respondents, there appeared to be higher levels of similarities in these characteristics between them and their parents, which may have facilitated the process of identification.

There has been little attention to the influence of primary figures, such as parents, on the development of roles in same-sex relationships. The assumption is made that it is difficult for gays and lesbians to identify with figures, including parents, who have a heterosexual orientation. In this study, the sexual orientation of parents was not a significant factor in identifying with them as relational role models. The sex and sexual orientation of parents were less important than their human qualities with which respondents identified and that they wished to emulate in their relationships with partners. Respondents talked of identifying selectively with admirable qualities perceived in parents.

Individuals who did not report similarities with one or both parents felt that their relationships with partners were more open to communication, less conflictual, less abusive, and more equitable than the marriages of their parents. As a consequence, they rejected parents as role models and looked elsewhere for figures of identification on which to develop their relationships.

Some gays and lesbians identified with other heterosexual couples as models for their relationships. These identifications were with specific qualities, such as kindness and commitment to a spouse, which partners admired and wished to adopt in their own relationships. Other gay and lesbian couples were mentioned by some individuals as influential models for developing roles in their relationships. Individuals who witnessed and identified with the successes of same-sex relationships were reassured that they, too, could have a successful relationship.

Compared to same-sex couples, heterosexual couples did not devote as much time and energy to negotiating marital roles because society had already framed "appropriate" role behavior in marriage. In fact, there was relatively little conflict among most heterosexual men and women in accepting the cultural ascriptions of gender roles in marriage that characterized the post–World War II era when most of them married. Society does not sanction the legitimacy of same-sex relationships, so there were few, if any, norms for structuring these relationships. As a consequence, same-sex partners reported lengthy periods of negotiation to work out roles associated with relational ambiguities. Several respondents felt unencumbered by stereotypical expectations and reported a sense of freedom in building relationships that met their individual and relational needs, a theme found in other studies of same-sex partners who rejected role models in developing their relationships (McWhirter and Mattison 1984; Blumstein and Schwartz 1983).

Within same-sex relationships, role behaviors between partners were shaped primarily by the talents and skills and, secondarily, by other factors such as personal interests and employment schedules. Both gays and lesbians rejected rigid expectations about relational behaviors, particularly those based on traditional gender stereotypes, which was comparable with other research (Blumstein and Schwartz 1983; Kurdek 1993; Maracek, Finn, and Cardell 1982; McWhirter and Mattison 1984; Tuller 1978).

An evolution of roles over the lifespan of these relationships characterized the interactions of partners, which resulted in adaptive shifts toward enhanced self-esteem and higher levels of relational satisfaction. The process of working out modifications in relational roles was different qualitatively for lesbians compared with gays and heterosexuals. Lesbians processed their experiences by discussing their thoughts and feelings in order to develop a mutual understanding that served as the basis for negotiating modifications in roles. Gay and heterosexual partners did not reflect as much as lesbians on their relationships in working out tasks and responsibilities that were mutually satisfying to each partner.

RELATIONAL FIT

Despite these fundamental differences about traditional and nontra-ditional roles, we found a high level of complementarity in the relation-ships of all couples. That is, respondents experienced themselves in relational roles as different from their spouses and partners. When respondents described how they and their partners fit together, more than 70 percent used language that suggested a complementary fit; for example, one person's behavior might be confrontational and the other's avoidant when there was conflict; one person might be talented at cooking and the other at managing finances. Compared with gays and heterosexual couples, more lesbians described themselves and their partners as different from each other in personal traits, relational styles, talents, and skills. Although some partners talked about their relation-ships as becoming more symmetrical in recent years, the complemen-tary fit remained constant for most respondents. During recent years, the complementary fit between heterosexual partners declined to six out of ten couples (from seven out of ten during the early years) but remained constant among nine out of ten lesbian and eight out of ten gay couples.

Complementarity has also been identified as important to relational stability and satisfaction in other studies (Kurdek 1993; McWhirter and Mattison 1984). Personal differences had the complementary function of enabling individuals to find qualities in their partners that were not part of themselves. As a consequence, individuals experienced a sense of wholeness that, they felt, would not have happened outside of relationships with their partners. Complementarity differences also provided relationships with resources so that tasks, especially household ones, were allocated equitably according to individual talents and skills. In same-sex relationships, it was common that one partner assume major responsibility for a task, such as cooking, while the other might take care of finances; in heterosexual relationships, tasks tended to be allocated along gender lines, with wives taking major responsibility for cooking and housework. Differences introduced novelty into relation-ships and helped to keep excitement alive after partners had been together for several years.

CONFLICT AND ITS MANAGEMENT

Complementarity, particularly in personality traits, had the potential to trigger major conflict between partners. When differences between spouses and partners were not discussed, especially those that a partner experienced as irritable, they had insidious effects on the quality of relationships. By the middle years, major conflict was reported by 47 percent of all respondents, which had doubled from the early years but dropped to 14 percent in recent years, as shown in figure 8.1. Over the years, major conflict was described more frequently by lesbians than by gays and heterosexuals: by the middle years, 58 percent of lesbian respondents reported major conflict compared to 46 percent of gays and 35 percent of heterosexuals. Although the increase in major conflict was attributed to several sources, the primary source was the avoidance of personal differences between partners, which began during the latter part of the early years. When issues that divided partners were not discussed openly and honestly, they had an undermining effect on the quality of relationships and often led to other serious relational difficulties, such as affairs with others, which were frequently reported by gay respondents.

Other researchers have observed the effects of how habitual avoidance of differences leads to unresolved tensions, which result in conflict that is distressing to individual partners and disruptive to relationships (Gottman 1994; Levinger 1979; Baucom, Notarius, Burnett, and Haefner 1990). Confronting conflict resulting from interpersonal differences tends to contribute to relational stability and satisfaction (Cahn

Figure 8.1
Major Conflict Reported by Heterosexual and Same-Sex Couples

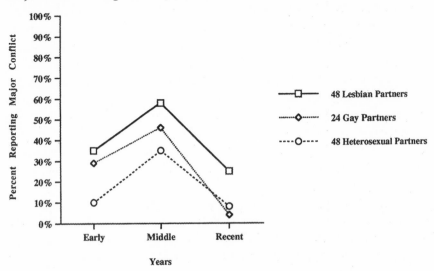

1990; Hendrick 1995). In our study, major conflict that was fed by avoidance in facing underlying feelings about the behavior(s) of a partner resulted in a decline in physical and psychological intimacy and compromised mutual trust, respect, and understanding.

Differences were apparent between men and women when they spoke about major conflict. We wonder if the finding of more women describing major conflict throughout their relationships suggested serious problems in their relationships or if it resulted from the orientation of women to discuss relational matters more openly than gays and heterosexual men. The propensity of lesbian partners to process their experiences may have resulted in more frequent identification of conflict between them compared with other respondents. Both lesbians and heterosexual women may have felt more comfortable than men in acknowledging the presence of serious conflict that men may have denied. In support of that hypothesis, 42 percent of heterosexual women compared with 29 percent of heterosexual men reported major conflict during the middle years.

Almost 60 percent of heterosexual women along with an equal ratio of gays were the least satisfied with their relationships during the middle years. Despite the level of major conflict in their relationships in the middle years, 42 percent of lesbians were satisfied with their relationships during that period. The reasons for unhappiness with relationships in the middle years differed for each group: heterosexual women expressed dissatisfaction with estrangements in marital relationships as a result of child rearing; gays were struggling with their commitments to partners, which were often threatened by sexual affairs; lesbians seemed to feel satisfaction with their lives together even when major conflict undermined relational stability. A major contributor to dissatisfaction was the avoidance of discussing feelings that respondents feared would threaten relationships. Paradoxically, the more partners avoided discussing their feelings about conflict, the more estranged and dissatisfied they became.

Compared to gay and heterosexual couples, lesbians, who were more avoidant than those two groups during the early years, progressed on a lineal path toward a confrontative style of managing interpersonal conflict that was characterized by face-to-face discussions of differences. Among heterosexual couples, husbands contributed disproportionately to the avoidant styles of these couples: 71 percent of heterosexual men and only 38 percent of their wives reported avoidant styles early in marriage. Lesbians and heterosexual men shared avoidant styles during the early years when 65 percent of lesbians and 71 percent of husbands avoided facing their partners with unpleasant feelings about their relationships. Although all partners became more confrontative during recent years, more than half of heterosexual men continued to avoid face-to-face discussions with their wives about difficulties in relationships.

The data suggested that confrontative modes of handling differences by women need to be understood within the context of relationships. In heterosexual relationships, women took a confrontative role with their husbands, who tended to be avoidant in managing conflict. In same-sex relationships, women avoided conflict yet gradually and persistently learned face-to-face modes of managing conflict as they moved through the middle and into the recent years. Avoidance among gay and heterosexual men was related, at least partly, to the ways in which males in our culture are socialized. Traditionally men have not been offered much support to resolve interpersonal conflict through face-to-face discussions. While women may be oriented from an early age to become skilled at relational matters, which may include conflict resolution, their relational orientation may become compromised when human fears of being abandoned take center stage. Among lesbians, there was significant fear early in relationships of losing their partners if irritable differences and dissatisfactions were confronted. In order to preserve relationships that were experienced as a very important aspect in the lives of most lesbian partners, direct and open discussion was avoided. Facing unpleasant and angry feelings that individuals feared would destroy their relationships was a mutual process in which both partners were involved. While many partners avoided confrontation by withdrawing into silence, others used words to obscure strong feelings even as they continued to discuss their experiences. The relational orientation of women in same-sex relationships was a valuable resource in adopting direct, face-to-face modes of handling differences during the middle and recent years.

An important barometer of the quality of relationships was in how partners reported their satisfaction with communication. Differences were apparent in the patterns of communication between partners from early to recent years. During the early years, more than half of all respondents reported significant difficulties in communicating with their partners, particularly heterosexual women, 75 percent of whom were not satisfied with the communication with their husbands. During the middle years, the assessment of heterosexual women about communicating with their partners improved somewhat, primarily because they had to discuss child rearing. Considerable regression was reported by gay partners in the middle years, while the quality of communication between lesbians remained at a similar level as the early years. In recent years, the quality of communication improved dramatically between lesbian partners and returned to the levels of the early years between gay partners. These communication patterns probably reflected the differences between men and women in relational skills. The centrality of relational attachments, which include skill at interpersonal communication, has been identified as a difference in how men and women are socialized to and oriented in relationships (Bergman 1991; Chodorow 1978; Gilligan 1982; Jordon 1986; Levant 1996; Surrey 1984). Our findings support that hypothesis.

One of the fortuitous aspects of this research was in discovering that many same-sex couples had sought psychotherapy for relational difficulties. A substantially higher ratio of lesbians compared with gays were involved in couples treatment. The orientation of lesbian couples toward processing their interpersonal experiences, along with their attunement to relational dynamics, offered us an opportunity to understand how psychotherapy worked for them. Their observations are valuable in thinking about the central elements in psychotherapy with same-sex as well as heterosexual couples who are troubled by relational difficulties.

Exploration, reflection, and acceptance of individual partners within the context of their relationships were important elements in the role of therapists as they worked with couples. Empathic understanding was the basis for supporting couples toward higher levels of adaptation. New learning about relationships, which included modifications in thinking and the adoption of new role behaviors, was possible once these elements became integrated into the therapeutic relationship. A supportive relationship was the vehicle for integrating new learning into relationships between partners, which became the basis for specific behavioral shifts.

RELATIONAL VALUES

Relational values of trust, respect, sensitivity, understanding, and equity gave meaning to roles and prevented differences from seriously damaging or destroying the connections between partners. Symmetry in underlying values was the glue that kept partners together when differences strained their connections.

There were differences between men and women in how they valued sensitivity and understanding. Women perceived themselves as sensitive and men as understanding, particularly during the early years of relationships. Those differences appeared to reflect how men and women valued being sensitive or understanding in a relationship. Men may have needed to see themselves as understanding in order to have a sense of control over interactions with their partners. Women were tolerant of the ambiguities of being with their partners and valued emotional attunement without necessarily needing to understand fully what was transpiring between them in relationships. Although heterosexual, gay, and lesbian partners reflected together on their relational experiences and learned to modify behaviors, women, especially lesbians, talked more extensively about the processing of their experiences. For lesbians, understanding emerged from the gradual process of becoming aware of and sensitive to their own and their partners' relational needs; this led to a sense of mutual empathy, which was identified as an important component in these lesbian relationships. These variations on the theme of understanding and sensitivity may reflect differences in the value orientations of men and women in relationships (Levant 1996).

The value of trust was framed differently by gays. For most gays, trust did not include monogamy. For heterosexuals and lesbians, trust was a matter of psychological availability along with sexual monogamy. As all partners lived out their lives together in recent years, they talked of trusting their partners to be available to them when they needed an accepting, supportive, and caring listener, someone to whom they could turn without feeling excessively uncomfortable.

A sense of equity about relationships was shaped by several factors. Differences in income were a primary source of inequity, especially among lesbian couples. Material and nonmaterial resources that partners contributed to and took from relationships needed to be perceived as balanced for lesbians to feel a sense of fairness about being together. Over the years, equity was a value that appeared more important to the stability and satisfaction in lesbian relationships than in other relationships. Between lesbian partners, much time was invested in processing differences that reflected the importance of preserving individual autonomy within meaningful relationships often characterized by inequity in material and nonmaterial resources. Gays talked less about negotiating matters that may have stimulated feelings of inequity. They attributed fairness to a fifty-fifty partnership that gays thought characterized their relationships over the years even when there were inequities in resources. Among heterosexual couples, the child-rearing years, or middle years, were experienced as the most inequitable, especially by women. By recent years, most heterosexual respondents felt that differences in tasks and responsibilities, which triggered feelings of inequity during the child-rearing years, were balanced by the mutual recognition and acceptance of resources each partner contributed to and took from relationships.

DECISION MAKING

An important dimension of understanding adaptation in these relationships was decision-making. There was not much difference between heterosexual and same-sex couples in the mutuality of making decisions.

There was a relatively steady path among lesbian couples toward greater mutuality in making decisions over the years; a similar pattern was found in the reports of heterosexual respondents. Despite avoidance of conflict, which fueled major conflict during the middle years, more than 70 percent of all couples reported jointly discussing impending decisions that affected them as a couple, for example, major purchases, choice of friends, and child rearing. While respondents talked positively about making decisions together, they expressed distress at avoiding underlying differences that led to major conflict in many relationships during the middle years. Mutuality in making decisions probably helped to stabilize relationships when partners were avoiding face-to-face discussions of differences.

One out of two lesbian couples in this study were parents who were rearing children. Motherhood was complicated by social policies, laws, and attitudes about same-sex parenthood. Decisions always had to be made within the context of laws and court rulings that were not supportive of same-sex couples, especially when they were parents. Heterosexual couples did not have to contend with the same issues when they considered parenthood. The investment in processing their relational experiences and skill at communication were valuable resources in helping lesbian couples make decisions about parenthood.

Decision making about managing finances, important in itself, was also symbolic of other dynamics in these relationships. Gays and heterosexuals tended to make decisions about money that focused on balancing contributions of partners to relationships. When incomes were very uneven, partners in these relationships looked to other kinds of contributions that promoted equity in relationships. As lesbians discussed the significance of incomes in their relationships and their ways of making decisions about spending money, themes of power, autonomy, mutuality, and equity emerged. The explicit connections several lesbian respondents made between these underlying dynamics and money resulted from the orientation of women to process their relational experiences. More than others, lesbians were oriented toward becoming sensitive to the significance of income differences to their relationships; gays and heterosexual partners were empirical in making decisions about finances and did not associate money with other dynamics. For lesbians, managing finances represented something about their life together that needed to be understood within the context of relationships as a whole. Through the years, lesbians spent more time than gays and heterosexuals in negotiating decisions related to the significance of uneven incomes in their relationships. Even among lesbian partners who had relatively equal incomes, dynamics related to equity, autonomy, and power became part of the process of making decisions about managing finances and spending money.

INTIMACY

Intimacy was the sense of communion between partners in the sexual, physical, and psychological dimensions of their relationships. Similarities were apparent in the quality of sexual relations among heterosexual, gay, and lesbian couples as they passed through the middle years and into the recent years of their relationships. Although sexual relations were less frequent and satisfying for lesbians, all couples had much in common in their assessments of sex, as figure 8.2 shows.

More than seven out of ten respondents were satisfied with the quality and frequency of sex in the early years; there was a relatively steady decline in this dimension of intimacy over the years. During the middle years, sexual relations were a barometer of the level of major conflict, which resulted in estrangement in these relationships. By recent years, about five out of ten couples did not assess their sexual relations in a positive way. Several interpretations were offered by respondents for this decline, which included a waning libido and interest in sex associated with growing older; several respondents,

Figure 8.2
Positive Sexual Relations among Heterosexual
and Same-Sex Couples

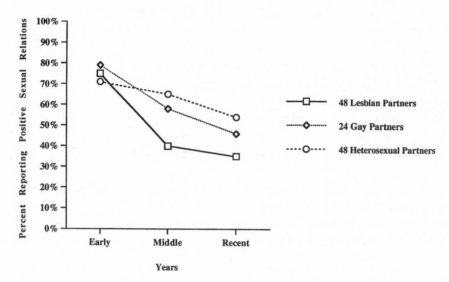

mostly heterosexuals, spoke of physical impairments that interfered with enjoying sexual relations.

The advent of HIV had a significant impact on sexual practices, especially among gay respondents. In addition to changing behaviors based on awareness of the dangers of unprotected sexual relations, this lethal virus has stimulated a reappraisal of many aspects of relationships (Aronson 1996). The story of two male partners who were infected with HIV ten years before this study, which is told in Chapter 6, was testimony to the adaptive capacities of human beings to transcend tragedy and not allow despair to rule their lives.

In contrast to sexual relations, the perceptions of psychological intimacy with one's partner grew significantly during recent years, as depicted in figure 8.3. In recent years, as the frequency and satisfaction with sex declined, psychological intimacy developed among most respondents; the development of personal closeness between partners served as a balance to the decline in sexual relations. Although sex continued to be seen as important from early through recent years, "the caring, the feeling, the understanding" that partners had for each other became even more important.

Figure 8.3
Psychological Intimacy among Heterosexual and Same-Sex Couples

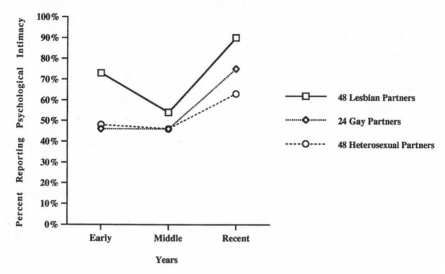

Physical closeness, which included hugging, touching, and cuddling, remained relatively constant over the years, although a slight decline was found in the middle years among same-sex couples, which was associated with estrangement in their relationships. Over the years, same-sex partners expressed their affection for each other through touching and hugging more than heterosexual spouses.

SOCIAL SUPPORTS

Social supports are important to people who are embarking on committed relationships. Marriage as a transition from one state to another calls on witnesses to support the newly married couple. Such social recognition and validation of relationships are not available to gay and lesbian couples, leading to challenges and stresses in their relationships different from those of heterosexual couples.

Of the potential sources of social support, family and religion were viewed as the least affirming and validating to gay and lesbian couples. A minority of families responded in an accepting way to the "news" that their adult son or daughter was a homosexual. Coming out as a gay or lesbian couple was usually the first explicit acknowledgment to a family of one's sexual orientation. Brothers and sisters of partners, many of whom were supportive, were often a valuable resource in the later rapprochement with parents. In recent years, however, fewer than half of their families were accepting of these relationships. Even when families expressed support, several of them experienced considerable underlying ambivalence manifested by forgetting the birthdays of partners or not including them in holiday celebrations. For heterosexual couples, the matter of family support for them and their marriages was "taken for granted." It was rarely so among lesbians and gays.

A similar theme was apparent as respondents talked about the significance of religion in their lives. Indifference or negative responses to traditional churches were frequently connected to past experiences with clergy and resulted in the marginal role of religion in the lives of most gay and lesbian respondents. Similar to heterosexual respondents, gays and lesbians expressed an interest in "spirituality," which was partly indicative of their struggles to retain a sense of integrity rather than despair about themselves and their lives as they negotiated the middle and older years.

Friends are an important source of social support for all committed couples. Although research on the positive significance of friends to same-sex couples is not consistent (Jones and Bates 1978; Kurdek and Schmitt 1985/86; Kurdek 1988b), most respondents in our study valued friendships, next to their relationships with their partners, as their most important source of individual and couple support. Friends of same-sex couples served as an extended family, which was important given the lack of support from most families. They were valued for acceptance, understanding, and validation of relationships; friends also helped to take the pressure off relationships during difficult times. Although many friendships began in relationships with individual partners, couple friendships became more common in recent years. Often the process of developing joint friends was associated with partners coming out and feeling confident about being identified as a same-sex couple.

CONCLUDING THOUGHTS

We have discussed similarities and variations in the lasting relationships of heterosexual, gay, and lesbian couples. Overall patterns from early through recent years in roles, relational fit, conflict and its management, decision making, and sexual and psychological intimacy were similar regardless of the sexual orientations of respondents.

Variations in these patterns appeared to be more a function of gender rather than sexual orientation. Certainly, interpretation of our findings needs to be framed in a way that respects the dynamic interplay of the orientations of men and women within the context of heterosexual and same-sex relationships. Unidimensional views that purport to present an accurate understanding of human beings as they live out their lives together fall short of appreciating the complexity and dynamism of heterosexual and same-sex relationships.

Women partners in same-sex relationships tended to be more tenacious than men or heterosexual women in processing their experiences together with the goal of enhancing acceptance, mutual empathy, and understanding. In fact, modifications in specific role behaviors resulted from the development of understanding between partners that was an outcome of processing their relational experiences. Partners were ready to work at modification of their roles to the extent that they experienced mutual support in the form of acceptance, empathy, and understanding. These women have much to teach us about the viability of relationships that last. Persistence at processing experiences reinforces commitment to relationships.

There has been considerable attention paid to the notion of fusion in lesbian relationships, which may be characterized by fluid boundaries and interpersonal enmeshment (Burch 1982; Krestan and Bepko 1980). Some authors have suggested that close emotional attachments among lesbian partners serve a protective function toward a society that is hostile to homosexuals and same-sex relationships (Mencher and Slater 1991). Others see fusion-like attachments as a functional characteristic of women's relationships (Green 1990; Mencher 1990). The lesbian relationships in our study were marked by autonomy within connectedness. Lesbian respondents rejected fusion as a distinguishing quality of their relationships while at the same time affirming the centrality of attachment to their partners (O'Rourke 1996; Reuman-Hemond 1994). They felt that personal independence within committed relationships was critical to individual well-being and to the viability of relationships. A sense of oneness may have complemented differences, which enabled partners to be psychologically connected while maintaining their individuality. Integration of personal autonomy within the intimacy of a committed relationship contributed to relational stability.

Lesbians and heterosexual men were similar in using avoidant styles of conflict management during the early years of relationships, although the dynamics that motivated those behaviors were different for each group. Heterosexual men did not seem "at home" with modes of conflict management that emphasized face-to-face discussion with their wives of unpleasant thoughts and feelings. For men, avoidance appeared to be fueled by the ways in which they are socialized in our culture. As a consequence, men internalized patterns of denial and avoidance that tended to persist over the years. Wives in heterosexual relationships employed confrontative modes of dealing with conflict with their husbands that were quite different from lesbians in same-sex relationships during the early years. Avoidance by lesbians during that time was a consequence of their fear of losing the most important relationship in their lives if they confronted conflict. The fear of abandonment was a powerful force promoting avoidance between lesbian partners during the early years of their relationships. Only as they persisted in processing their experiences did lesbian partners begin to feel confident about confronting each other with thoughts and feelings that previously had been intimidating to them. For most lesbian partners, couples psychotherapy was a valuable resource in their quest for happiness with each other.

Major conflict, which was reported more frequently by lesbians than by gays and heterosexuals, was not in itself a reliable indicator of relational stability and satisfaction. Lesbians may not only have been aware of the presence of major conflict but more accepting and tolerant of it because of their orientation to processing their relational experiences. Perhaps their high rates of involvement in couples psychotherapy enabled them to understand and accept the presence of conflict. Women in committed relationships with each other may have less "need" to deny major conflict as they develop modes of confronting differences in the middle years and beyond.

The development of psychological intimacy characterized all these relationships as couples negotiated their paths through the middle and recent years. Psychological intimacy was important as a balance to the decline in the quality and satisfaction with sexual relations. Psychological intimacy enhanced personal well-being among respondents and was a positive reinforcement for commitment to relationships. These respondents made an eloquent case for all couples in cultivating a relationship in which a partner became one's "best friend" through the middle and senior years of life.

The staying power of relational values—trust, respect, sensitivity, understanding, and equity—cannot be underestimated in understanding how these relationships lasted for so many years. These core values provided continuity in relationships during stressful times, especially during the middle years. The symmetry and mutuality in relational values enabled partners to maintain their commitments to each other.

In the Preface to this book, we stated that our goal was to promote sensitivity and understanding toward gay and lesbian relationships that last. We believe that one of the more effective ways of realizing that goal and of neutralizing the social ills of oppression and prejudice directed toward lesbians and gays is through human understanding. These same-sex partners spoke eloquently about their relationships. We hope that people who read our discussions of their stories will be as touched as we were by their commitments and struggles to build a meaningful life together.

Appendix A: Methodology

The research on which this book is based is part of our studies of adult relationships that last and also includes marriage (Mackey and O'Brien 1995). Similar to our other studies, the study of same-sex relationships used a qualitative and phenomenological approach to study the histories of seventy-two partners (respondents) from thirty-six relationships that had lasted at least fifteen years. An interview format was developed after a review of the research literature; the semistructured interview was pretested by the researchers. Collaborative researchers conducted additional pilot testing and provided feedback that led to further refinement of the interview guide. The guide was divided into four major sections: the relationship, social influences including economic and cultural factors, their parents' marriages, and respondents' experiences and views of their relationships over time, which was subdivided into the early years, the middle years, and the recent years. The objective was to acquire in-depth information from the perspectives of individual partners in order to develop an understanding of how they adapted over the life span of their relationships.

An open-ended style of interviewing was followed in order to allow for freedom of expression (Kvale 1983). Focal questions were used to elicit information from the unique perspectives of each respondent.

Interviews allowed for flexibility and openness; they were exploratory and discovery-oriented (Moon, Dillon, and Sprenkle 1990; Strauss and Corbin 1990), which allowed respondents to express the meanings and processes of their interactions within their own frame of reference. That approach, which adapted clinical interviewing skills to the needs of the research, allowed the researchers to explore the experiences of individual partners as they remembered and reported them.

The interviewers were advanced doctoral students with extensive clinical experience. They were sensitive to and respectful of respondents and accepting of the uniqueness of each individual's perceptions. Their empathic interviewing skills were a valuable resource in collecting the data.

The interviews were held in the homes of the respondents, which provided additional information about their lifestyles and environments. Prior to each interview, respondents were told about the purpose of the study, given an overview of the interview schedule, and assured that their identities would remain anonymous. Informed consent for audio taping and the research use of interviews was obtained. Each partner was interviewed separately; the length of each of the interviews was approximately two hours.

SAMPLE

The sample was chosen to fit with the goal of developing an understanding of adaptation between partners in long-lasting relationships. Criteria for inclusion were that same-sex partners be together a minimum of fifteen years and that both be willing participants. Volunteers were recruited through local churches, recreational and social groups, gay and lesbian newspapers, as well as flyers posted in bookstores. The researchers employed snowball sampling techniques through which respondents identified other potential participants. Such an approach has been used successfully in other studies with similar populations (Johnson 1991; Reilly and Lynch 1990). The sample consisted of gays and lesbians without children and lesbians with children.

Seventy-two respondents from thirty-six relationships were interviewed. Twenty-four respondents were gay men and forty-eight were lesbians. By age, 50 percent of respondents were in their forties, 26 percent in their fifties, and 24 percent were sixty years or over. Ninety-seven percent of couples had been together from sixteen to twenty-nine years and 3 percent from thirty to thirty-nine years. Of the twelve lesbian couples who were rearing children, two thirds had two children or less and one third had three children or more. The religious background of 33 percent of the sample was Catholic, 49 percent Protestant, and 18 percent Jewish. Joint incomes of couples were distributed as follows: 15 percent under $50,000; 35 percent from $50,000 to $100,000; 31 percent over $100,000. Eighteen percent of respondents had some college or less, and 82 percent had at least a college degree.

CODING AND DATA ANALYSIS

Each taped interview was transcribed to facilitate coding and to prepare the data for both quantitative and qualitative analysis. Data was classified and analyzed using the "grounded theory" method (Strauss and Corbin 1990). The transcribed data was coded line by line for key themes and developed into categories.

Based on procedures developed earlier in the lasting relationships research, transcriptions were coded blindly by a research team of two raters (one woman, one man). Detailed notes were kept, and categories were generated. A relationship coding sheet that labeled categories was developed. As new categories arose, previous interviews were recoded in keeping with the constant comparative process. Having both genders involved added to the strength of the coding and contributed to the development of a shared conceptual analysis. Using this method, a scoring system was developed to identify themes that evolved from each section of the interviews. There were more than ninety categories in twenty-four topic areas for every respondent; rating scores were developed for each of the three time periods of their relationships (early, middle, and recent years), which were marked approximately at five-year intervals (see Chapter 1 for a discussion of how we defined these time frames).

One of the authors coded all seventy-two interviews to insure continuity in the operational definitions of variables and consistency of judgments from case to case. The raters then met to review their independent codes. When discrepancies occurred, the raters discussed the differences and referred to the original transcript until consensus was reached as to how a particular item should be scored. The inter-rater reliability was .86.

Once the interviews were coded, the data from the scoring sheets were analyzed using the Statistical Package for the Social Sciences software (SPSS). Nonparametric statistics enabled the research team to identify significant patterns of stability and change in relationships over time. Chi square analyses were used to examine the relationships between the independent variables of sexual orientation and the dependent variables of roles, relational fit, relational values, decision making, conflict, styles of managing conflict, sexual relations, physical and psychological intimacy, social supports, and satisfaction with relationships. The Alpha criteria was set at .05.

Quantitative analysis offered direction to the qualitative analysis. The latter included the use of Hyper Research software (Hesse-Biber, Dupuis, and Kinder 1992), which enabled the researchers to identify, catalogue, and organize specific interview passages on which quantitative codes had been based. Hyper research was a highly efficient and reliable tool in the qualitative analysis of data. The software allowed us to do a thorough content analysis of the seventy-two transcriptions of taperecorded interviews that totaled approximately three thousand double-spaced pages.

Appendix B: Interview Guide

INTRODUCTION

- Thank you for being in the study.
- Brief explanation of the project.
- Read and sign consent form.
- Complete background information.
- Explain structure of the interview:

1. Your relationship as it was when you first identified yourselves as a committed couple and how it has stayed the same as well as how it has changed in terms of roles, expectations, and needs.
2. A look at your own family background, values, and sociocultural context over time and how these influenced your relationship.
3. The influence of your parents' marriage or other significant relationships on your own relationship in terms of roles, expectations, and relating.
4. Your assessment of the important factors in your relationship over time.

INTERVIEW

I. The Relationship

A. Initial attraction, life circumstances, family reactions.

   1. As you look back to the time when you met (partner), what first attracted you to (partner)? What do you think attracted (partner) to you?

      a. What interests did you share?

      b. How did you know when you were committed to each other? Was this understood to be a lifelong commitment? How was that understood?

      c. How long were you together before making the decision to commit to each other? If a short time, how were you sure?

   2. How did your family feel toward, react to, and treat (partner)?

      a. How does your family understand your relationship?

      b. Tell me about your family's reaction to your committed relationship (feelings of approval or disapproval).

      c. How does this reaction vary among family members?

   3. How did (partner's) family react to your committed relationship?

   4. What was going on in your life around the time you committed to each other—educationally, vocationally, personally, family, etc.

   5. What kinds of roles, particular functions, or talents did you see yourself bringing into the relationship?

      a. What about (partner's) role? (Expected, actual, changes).

      b. Did you expect to have to work at the relationship? Why?

   6. What, if any, adjustments did you have to make in the initial stages of your committed relationship? Feelings about these changes? What adjustments did (partner) have to make?

B. Roles, expectations, problem solving. Issues of satisfaction, relatedness, and equity in the beginning (one–five years), in the middle (five–ten years), and most recently (after ten years). Ask how each thing changed over time.

   1. Can you tell me how you and (partner) got along?

      a. In general?

      b. How would you describe the communication between you?

      c. How have you gotten along sexually? How important has sex been to your relationship over time?

      d. How have you gotten along in terms of nonsexual intimacy, physical affection like touching and hugging?

      e. What has been important to getting along? (e.g., sense of humor? talking it through? allowing space?)

   2. How did you go about making decisions and solving problems? (re: work, friends, recreation, etc.)?

    a. How did you handle differences (values, career, sex, etc.)?

    b. How would you describe your problem-solving style as compared to your partner's?

    c. Is there one particular area of conflict that stood out during each of the three phases of your relationship?

    d. Can you give me some examples of how you faced and dealt with crises (health, financial, interpersonal conflicts, etc.)?

3. How have you felt about your relationship?

    a. What's been good, not so good, and/or bad about the relationship?

    b. How much understanding did you feel (partner) had of you? (differentiation, separateness, etc.)

    c. How much understanding did you have of (partner)?

    d. How sensitive was (partner) to you? And you to (partner)?

    e. How much respect did you feel (partner) had for you? And you for (partner)?

    f. How much trust did you feel toward (partner)?

    g. How much trust did you think (partner) felt toward you?

4. Overall, how much of a sense of fairness did you feel in the relationship?

    a. Despite differences, did things balance out?

    b. Do you feel that your ways of solving problems as a couple were generally fair to each partner?

    c. Were there situations where one of you had more influence than the other? (money, friends, recreation, work, etc.)

5. What do you identify as transition points in your relationship? How would you describe various phases of your relationship?

6. Have you ever been in individual therapy? Have you ever been in therapy to address concerns in this relationship?

II. Socioeconomic and Cultural Influences

How have the following played a part in your life together, and how have they affected your relationship?

A. Religion

B. Extended families

    1. How have cousins, aunts, uncles, etc. impacted on your relationship?

    2. What relationships have you had to a gay/lesbian community or organization? Friends? How have those impacted?

C. Cultural factors including ethnicity, race, and sexual orientation

    1. How have homophobia, social pressures, and failures to recognize you as a couple drawn you closer or been divisive in your relationship?

    2. How have societal attitudes affected your relationship over time?

    3. How have your ethnic and/or racial backgrounds impacted?

D. Economic factors, including income

E. Other values, beliefs, moral standards, or a motto that fits for you

III. Parents' Marriage and Influence of Other Significant Relationships

A. What were family attitudes toward/experience with the breakup of a committed relationship? What attitudes would you expect from family if your current relationship were to dissolve?

B. What models of relationships did you look to to construct your idea of a committed relationship? What one was most significantly influential? (If response is "parents," skip to no. 2.)

    1. What did you learn about long-term relationships from this model?

        a. How did you view this model in terms of roles, relatedness, and equity?

        b. Can you tell me how the partners in this couple got along?

        c. How did they go about making decisions and solving problems? (Ask for some examples of how a disagreement was solved.)

        d. Overall, was there a sense of fairness in their relationship? Despite differences, did things balance out in their relationship? Did you feel that their ways of solving problems were generally fair to each partner? Were there situations where one of them had more influence than the other? (money, friends, recreation, work)

    2. What do you think you learned about committed relationships from observing your parents?

        a. How did you view your parents' relationship in terms of roles, relatedness, and equity?

        b. Can you tell me how your parents got along?

        c. How did they go about making decisions and solving problems? (Ask for some examples of how a disagreement was solved.)

        d. Overall, how much of a sense of fairness was there in their relationship? Despite differences, did things balance out in their relationship? Did you feel that their ways of solving problems were generally fair to each partner? Were there situations where one of them had more influence than the other? (money, friends, recreation, work)

   e. What are some important similarities in your relationship compared to your parents' marriage? What are some important differences?

IV. Participants Views of the Relationship over Time and Wrap Up

A. Factors that kept you in the relationship

   1. As you look back, what were the personal qualities of (partner) that kept you together?

   2. What personal qualities of yours kept you together?

   3. What other factors in the relationship kept you together?

B. Changes

   1. Do you think your relationship has changed, or has the relationship remained pretty much the same from the beginning?

   2. How have your expectations changed or remained the same?

   3. How does what you are currently looking for in the relationship differ from earlier expectations? (needs, roles, relatedness, communication)

C. What words best describe what (partner) means to you now? In the past?

D. Are there any other things that you wish to add that were critical issues/factors that kept you in the relationship? Significant events, periods of assessment, and/or renewal?

E. Is there anything else that you think would be important for me to understand about your relationship, yourself, or your partner?

Thank you!

Bibliography

Aronson, J. (1996). Relationship stability: A qualitative psychological study of long term gay male couples. Unpublished doctoral dissertation, Boston College, Boston, Mass.

Barrows, P. A., and Halgin, R. P. (1988). Current issues in psychotherapy with gay men: Impact of the AIDS phenomenon. *Professional Psychology: Research and Practice* 19 (4): 395–402.

Baucom, D. H., Notarius, C. I., Burnett, C. K., and Haefner, P. (1990). Gender differences and sex role identity in marriage. In F. D. Fincham and T. N. Bradbury (eds.), *The psychology of marriage: Basic issues and applications* (pp. 150–171). New York: Guilford.

Berger, R. M. (1990a). Men together: Understanding the gay couple. *Journal of Homosexuality* 19 (3): 31–49.

———. (1990b). Passing: Impact on the quality of same-sex couple relationships. *Social Work* 35 (4): 328–32.

Bergman, S. (1991). *Men's psychological development: A relational perspective.* Work in Progress, no. 48. Wellesley Mass.: Stone Center Working Paper Series.

Berzon, B. (1992). Building successful relationships. In B. Berzon (ed.), *Positively gay: New approaches to gay and lesbian life.* Berkeley, Calif.: Celestial Arts.

Blasband, D., and Peplau, L. A. (1985). Sexual exclusivity versus sexual openness in gay male couples. *Archives of Sexual Behavior* 14 (5): 395–412.

Blumenfeld, W. J., and Raymond, D. (1993). *Looking at gay and lesbian life*. Boston: Beacon Press.

Blumstein, P., and Schwartz, P. (1983). *American couples: Money, work, sex*. New York: William Morrow and Company, Inc.

———. (1989). Intimate relationships and the creation of sexuality. In B. J. Risman and P. Schwartz (eds.), *Gender in intimate relationships* (pp. 120–29). Belmont, Calif.: Wadsworth.

Bozett, F. W. (1993). Gay fathers: A review of the literature. In L. D. Garnets and D. C. Kimmel (eds.), *Psychological perspectives on lesbian and gay male experiences* (pp. 437–58). New York: Columbia University Press.

Broderick, J. E., and O'Leary, K. D. (1986). Contributions of affect, attitudes, and behavior to marital satisfaction. *Journal of Consulting and Clinical Psychology* 54: 514–17.

Brown, L. S. (1989). New voices, new visions: Toward a lesbian/gay paradigm for psychology. *Psychology of Women Quarterly* 13: 445–58.

Bullough, V. (1979). *Homosexuality: A history from Ancient Greece to gay liberation*. New York: New American Library.

Burch, B. (1982). Psychological merger in lesbian couples: A joint ego psychological and systems approach. *Family Therapy* 9: 201–8.

———. (1986). Psychotherapy and the dynamics of merger in lesbian couples. In T. S. Stein and C. J. Cohen (eds.), *Contemporary perspectives on psychotherapy with lesbians and gay men*. New York: Plenum Medical.

———. (1993). *On intimate terms: The psychology of difference in lesbian relationships*. Chicago: University of Illinois Press.

Burke, R. J., Weier, T., and Harrison, D. (1976). Disclosure of problems and tensions experienced by marital problems. *Psychological Reports* 38: 531–42.

Cahn, D. (1990). Confrontation behaviors, perceived understanding, and relationship growth. In D. Cahn (ed.), *Intimates in conflict* (pp. 153–65). Hillsdale, N.J.: Erlbaum.

Caldwell, M., and Peplau, L. A. (1984). The balance of power in lesbian relationships. *Sex Roles* 10: 587–99.

Campbell, S. M. (1980). *The couple's journey: Intimacy as a path to wholeness*. San Luis Obispo (Calif.): Impact Publishers.

Cardell, M., Finn, S., and Maracek, J. (1981). Sex-role identity, sex-role behavior, and satisfaction in heterosexual, lesbian, and gay male couples. *Psychology of Women Quarterly* 5 (3): 488–94.

Carl, D. (1986). Acquired Immune Deficiency Syndrome: A preliminary examination of the effects on gay couples and coupling. *Journal of Marital and Family Therapy* 12 (3): 241–47.

————. (1990). *Counseling same-sex couples.* New York: Norton.

Chodorow, N. (1978). *The reproduction of mothering: Psychoanalysis and the sociology of gender.* Berkeley: University of California Press.

Clunis, D. M., and Green, G. D. (1993). *Lesbian couples.* Seattle: Seal Press.

Cole, C. L. (1985). Relationship quality in long-term marriages: A comparison of high quality and low quality marriages. *Lifestyles: A Journal of Changing Patterns* 7 (4): 248–57.

DeCecco, J. P., and Shively, M. G. (1978). A study of perceptions of rights and needs in interpersonal conflicts in homosexual relationships. *Journal of Homosexuality* 3 (3): 205–16.

D'Emilio, J. (1983). *Sexual politics, sexual communities: The making of a homosexual minority in the United States, 1940–1970.* Chicago: University of Chicago Press.

Demment, C. C. (1991). Marital satisfaction: A qualitative analysis. Unpublished doctoral dissertation, Boston College, Boston, Mass.

Dorn, B. I. (1991). An investigation into factors that contribute to successful long-term lesbian relationships. Unpublished doctoral dissertation, The Union Institute, Union, N.Y.

Driggs, J. H., and Finn, S. E. (1990). *Intimacy between men: How to find and keep gay love relationships.* New York: Dutton.

Duffy, S. M., and Rusbult, C. E. (1986). Satisfaction and commitment in homosexual and heterosexual relationships. *Journal of Homosexuality* 12 (2): 1–23.

Eichenbach, L., and Orbach, S. (1988). *Between women.* New York: Viking.

Eldridge, N. S., and Gilbert, L. A. (1990). Correlates of relationship satisfaction in lesbian couples. *Psychology of Women Quarterly* 14: 43–62.

Elise, D. (1986). Lesbian couples: The implications of sex differences in separation-individuation. *Psychotherapy* 23 (2): 305–10.

Erikson, E. (1950). *Childhood and society.* New York: W. W. Norton.

Faderman, L. (1991). *Odd girls and twilight lovers: A history of lesbian life in twentieth-century America.* New York: Penguin.

Falk, P. J. (1993). Lesbian mothers: Psychosocial assumptions in family law. In L. D. Garnets and D. C. Kimmel (eds.), *Psychological perspectives on lesbian and gay male experiences* (pp. 420–36). New York: Columbia University Press.

Forstein, M. (1984). AIDS anxiety in the "worried well." In S. Nichols and D. Ostrow (eds.), *Psychiatric implications of acquired immune deficiency syndrome* (pp. 50–60). Washington, D.C.: American Psychiatric Press.

————— . (1993). Psychotherapy with gay male couples: Loving in the time of AIDS. In S. A. Cadwell, R. A. Burnham, and M. Forstein (eds.), *Therapists on the front line: Psychotherapy with gay men in the age of AIDS* (pp. 293–315). Washington, D.C.: American Psychiatric Press.

Garnets, L., Herek, G. M., and Levy, B. (1993). Violence and victimization of lesbians and gay men: Mental health consequences. In L. D. Garnets and D. C. Kimmel (eds.), *Psychological perspectives on lesbian and gay male experiences* (pp. 579–97). New York: Columbia University Press.

Geis, S. B., Fuller, R. L., and Rush, J. (1986). Lovers of AIDS victims: Psychosocial stresses and counseling needs. *Death Studies* 10: 43–53.

George, K. D., and Behrendt, A. E. (1987). Therapy for male couples experiencing relationship problems and sexual problems. *Journal of Homosexuality* 14 (1–2): 77–88.

Gilligan, C. (1982). *In a different voice: Psychological theory and women's development.* Cambridge, (Mass.): Harvard University Press.

Glenn, N. D. (1990). Quantitative research on marital quality in the 1980's: A critical review. *Journal of Marriage and the Family* 52: 818–31.

Gonsiorek, J. C. (1988). Current and future directions in gay/lesbian affirmative mental health practice. In M. Shernoff and W. A. Scott (eds.), *Sourcebook on lesbian/gay health care* (pp. 107–13). Washington, D.C.: National Lesbian and Gay Health Foundation.

Gonsiorek, J. C., and Weinrich, J. D. (1991). *Homosexuality: Social, psychological, and biological issues.* Newbury Park, (Calif.): Sage.

Goode, W. J. (1962). Marital satisfaction and instability: A cross-cultural analysis of divorce rates. *International Social Science Journal* 14: 507–26.

Gottman, J. M. (1991). Predicting the longitudinal course of marriages. *Journal of Marital and Family Therapy* 17: 3–7.

————— . (1994). *Why marriages succeed or fail.* New York: Simon & Schuster.

Gray-Little, B., and Burks, N. (1983). Power and satisfaction in marriage: A review and critique. *Psychological Bulletin* 93: 513–38.

Green, G. D. (1990). Is separation really so great? *Women and Therapy* 9(1–2): 87–104.

Hamel, C. (1993). Factors involved in marital stability: A qualitative study of Afro-American couples. Unpublished doctoral dissertation, Boston College, Boston, Mass.

Harowski, K. J. (1987). The worried well: Maximizing coping in the face of AIDS. *Journal of Homosexuality* 14 (1): 299–306.

Harry, J. (1983). Decision making and age differences among gay male couples. *Journal of Homosexuality* 8 (2): 9–21.

————. (1984). *Gay couples.* New York: Praeger.

Hendrick, S. S. (1995). *Close relationships: What couple therapists can learn.* Pacific Grove, Calif: Brooks/Cole.

Herek, G. M., Kimmel, D. C., Amaro, H., and Melton, G. B. (1991). Avoiding heterosexist bias in psychological research. *American Psychologist* 46 (9): 957–63.

Hesse-Biber, S., Dupuis, P., and Kinder, T. S. (1992). HyperRESEARCH: A tool for the analysis of qualitative data. (computer program). Randolph, (Mass.): Researchware.

Hirsch, D., and Enlow, R. (1984). The effect of the acquired immune deficiency syndrome on gay lifestyle and the gay individual. *Annals of the New York Academy of the Sciences* 437: 273–82.

Hite, S. (1987). *Women and love: A cultural revolution in progress.* New York: Alfred A. Knopf.

Howard, J. A., Blumstein, P., and Schwartz, P. (1986). Sex, power, and influence tactics in intimate relationships. *Journal of Personality and Social Psychology* 51 (1): 102–9.

————. (1987). Social or evolutionary theories? Observations in human mate selection. *Journal of Personality and Social Psychology* 53: (1), 194–200.

Huston, T. L., and Ashmore, R. D. (1986). Women and men in personal relationships. In R. D. Ashmore and F. Del Boco (eds.), *The social psychology of female-male relations* (pp. 167–210). New York: Academic Press.

Johnson, S. E. (1991). *Staying power: Long term lesbian couples.* Tallahassee, (Fla.): The Naiad Press, Inc.

Jones, R. W., and Bates, J. E. (1978). Satisfaction in male homosexual couples. *Journal of Homosexuality* 3 (3): 217–24.

Jordon, J. (1986). *The meaning of mutuality.* Work in Progress, no. 23. Wellesley, Mass.: Stone Center Working Paper Series.

Joseph, J., Emmons, E., Kessler, R., Wortman, C., O'Brien, K., Hocher, W., and Schafer, C. (1984). Coping with the threat of aids: An approach to psychosocial assessment. *American Psychologist* 39: 1303–8.

Kaiser, C. (1994). Life before Stonewall. *Newsweek,* 4 July, 78–79.

Kanter, L. (1994). Marital stability: A qualitative study of Jewish couples. Unpublished doctoral dissertation, Boston College, Boston, Mass.

Kelley, D., and Burgoon, J. (1991). Understanding marital satisfaction and couple type as functions of relational expectations. *Human Communication Research* 18 (1): 40–69.

Kelley, H. H., and Thibault, J. W. (1978). *Interpersonal relations: A theory of interdependence.* New York: Wiley.

Kelly, E. L., and Conley, J. J. (1987). Personality and compatibility: A projective analysis of marital stability and marital satisfaction. *Journal of Personality and Social Psychology* 52: 27–40.

Kennedy, E. L., and Davis, M. D. (1993). *Boots of leather, slippers of gold.* New York: Penguin.

Kinsey, A. C., Pomeroy, W. B., and Martin, C. E. (1948). *Sexual behavior in the human male.* Philadelphia: W. B. Saunders.

Kinsey, A. C., Pomeroy, W. B., Martin, C. E., and Gebhard, D. (1953). *Sexual behavior in the human female.* Philadelphia: W. B. Saunders.

Krestan, J., and Bepko, C. S. (1980). The problem of fusion in the lesbian relationship. *Family Process* 19: 277–89.

Kurdek, L. A. (1988a). Relationship quality of gay and lesbian cohabiting couples. *Journal of Homosexuality* 15(3–4): 93–118.

———. (1988b). Perceived social support in gays and lesbians in cohabiting relationships. *Journal of Personality and Social Psychology* 54 (3): 504–9.

———. (1991a). Correlates of relationship satisfaction in cohabiting gay and lesbian couples: Integration of contextual, investment, and problem-solving models. *Journal of Personality and Social Psychology* 61(6): 910–22.

———. (1991b). The dissolution of gay and lesbian couples. *Journal of Social and Personal Relationships* 8: 265–78.

———. (1991c). Sexuality in homosexual and heterosexual couples. In K. McKinney and S. Sprecher (eds.), *Sexuality in close relationships* (pp. 177–91). Hillsdale, N.J.: Lawrence Erlbaum.

———. (1992). Relationship stability and relationship satisfaction in cohabiting gay and lesbian couples: A prospective longitudinal test of the contextual and interdependence models. *Journal of Social and Personal Relationships* 9: 125–42.

———. (1993). The allocation of household labor in gay, lesbian, and heterosexual married couples. *Journal of Social Issues* 49 (3): 127–39.

Kurdek, L. A., and Schmitt, J. P. (1985/86). Relationship quality of gay men in closed or open relationships. *Journal of Homosexuality* 12 (2): 85–99.

———. (1986). Relationship quality of partners in heterosexual married, heterosexual cohabiting, and gay and lesbian relationships. *Journal of Personality and Social Psychology* 51 (4): 711–20.

———. (1987a). Partner homogamy in married, heterosexual cohabiting, gay and lesbian couples. *Journal of Sex Research* 23(2): 212–32.

———. (1987b). Perceived emotional support from family and friends in members of homosexual, married, and heterosexual cohabiting couples. *Journal of Homosexuality* 14(3–4): 57–68.

Kvale, S. (1983). The qualitative research interview: A phenomenological and a hermeneutical mode of understanding. *Journal of Phenomenological Psychology* 14: 171–96.

Lauer, R. H., and Lauer, J. C. (1986). Factors in long-term marriages. *Journal of Family Issues* 7: 382–90.

Lauer, R. H., Lauer, J. C., and Kerr, S. T. (1990). The long-term marriage: Perceptions of stability and satisfaction. *International Journal of Aging and Human Development* 31: 189–95.

Lee, J. A. (1990). Can we talk? Can we really talk? Communication as a key factor in the maturing homosexual couple. *Journal of Homosexuality* 20 (3–4): 143–68.

Levant, R. (1996). The new psychology of men. *Professional Psychology: Research and Practice* 27: 259–69.

Lever, J. (1976). Sex differences in the games children play. *Social Problems* 23: 478–87.

Levine, M. (1979). *Gay men: The sociology of male homosexuality.* New York: Harper & Row.

Levinger, G. (1979). Marital cohesiveness at the brink: The fate of applications for divorce. In G. Levinger and O. C. Moles (eds.), *Divorce and separation.* Westport, Conn.: Praeger.

Lewis, R. A. and Spanier, G. B. (1979). Theorizing about the quality and stability of marriage. In W. Burr, L. Nye, R. Hill and I Reiss (eds.), *Contemporary theories about the family* pp. (268–94). Glencoe, Ill: The Free Press.

Loulan, J. (1984). *Lesbian sex.* San Francisco: Spinsters Ink.

Lynch, J. M., and Reilly, M. E. (1986). Role relationships: Lesbian perspectives. *Journal of Homosexuality* 12 (2): 53–70.

Mackey, R. A. (1985). *Ego Psychology and Clinical Practice.* New York: Gardner Press, Inc.

Mackey, R. A., and O'Brien, B. A. (1995). *Lasting marriages: Men and women growing together.* Westport, Conn.: Praeger.

——— . (1996a). Marital conflict management: Gender and ethnic differences. *Social Work* (in press).

——— . (1996b). Curvilinearity in marital relationships: A different prospective. Unpublished manuscript.

Maracek, J., Finn, S. E., and Cardell, M. (1982). Gender roles in the relationships of lesbians and gay men. *Journal of Homosexuality* 8(2): 45–49.

Martin, D., and Lyon, P. (1983). *Lesbian woman.* New York: Bantam.

McKenzie, S. (1992). Merger in lesbian relationships. *Women and Therapy* 12 (1–2): 151–60.

McWhirter, D. P. (1990). Prologue. In D. P. McWhirter, S. A. Sanders, and J. M. Reinisch (eds.), *Homosexuality/heterosexuality: Concepts of sexual orientation* (pp. xvi–xvii). New York: Oxford University Press.

McWhirter, D. P., and Mattison, A. M. (1984). *The male couple: How relationships develop.* Englewood Cliffs, N.J.: Prentice-Hall.

———. (1988). Psychotherapy for gay male couples. In J. DeCecco (ed.), *Gay relationships.* New York: Harrington Park Press.

Mencher, J. (1990). *Intimacy in lesbian relationships: A critical re-examination of fusion.* Work in Progress, no. 42. Wellesley, Mass.: Stone Center Working Paper Series.

Mencher, J., and Slater, S. (1991). New perspectives on the lesbian family experience. Paper presented at the annual convention of the Association for Women in Psychology, Hartford, Conn.

Mengden, S. (1994). Marital stability: A qualitative study of Mexican American couples. Unpublished doctoral dissertation, Boston College, Boston, Mass.

Miller, J. B. (1976). *Toward a new psychology of women.* Boston: Beacon Press.

———. (1984). *The development of women's sense of self.* Work in Progress, no. 12. Wellesley, Mass.: Stone Center Working Paper Series.

Moon, S., Dillon, D., and Sprenkle, D. (1990). Family therapy and qualitative research. *Journal of Marital and Family Therapy* 16: 357–73.

Morin, S. F. (1977). Heterosexual bias in psychological research on lesbianism and male homosexuality. *American Psychologist* 32: 629–37.

———. (1991). Removing the stigma: Lesbian and gay affirmative counseling. *Counseling Psychologist* 19 (2): 245–47.

Morin, S. F., Charles, K. A., & Malyon, A. K. (1984). The psychological impact of AIDS on gay men. *American Psychologist* 39 (11): 1288–93.

Nichols, M. (1988). Low sexual desire in lesbian couples. In S. Leiblum and R. Rosen (eds.), *Sexual desire disorders* (pp. 387–412). New York: Guilford Press.

Norton, A. J., and Moorman, J. E. (1987). Current trends in marriage and divorce among American women. *Journal of Marriage and the Family* 49: 3–14.

O'Brien, B., and Mackey, R. (1990a). Marital stability: Interview guide. Unpublished document, Boston College, Boston, Mass.

———. (1990b). Marital stability: Scoring system. Unpublished document, Boston College, Boston, Mass.

O'Rourke, J. (1996). Relational stability in lesbian couples with children: A qualitative psychological study. Unpublished doctoral dissertation, Boston College, Boston, Mass.

Peplau, L. A. (1981). What homosexuals want. *Psychology Today,* March, 28–38.

————. (1982). Research on homosexual couples: An overview. *Journal of Homosexuality* 8 (2): 3–8.

————. (1991). Lesbian and gay relationships. In J. C. Gonsiorek and J. D. Weinrich (eds.), *Homosexuality: Research implications for public policy* (pp. 177–96). Newbury Park, Calif.: Sage.

Peplau, L. A., and Amaro, H. (1982). Understanding lesbian relationships. In W. Paul, J. D. Weinrich, J. C. Gonsiorek, and M. E. Hotvedt (eds.), *Homosexuality: Social, psychological, and biological Issues* (pp. 233–47). Beverly Hills: Sage.

Peplau, L. A., Cochran, S., Rook, K., and Padesky, C. (1978). Loving women: Attachment and autonomy in lesbian relationships. *Journal of Social Issues* 34 (3): 7–27.

Peplau, L. A., and Cochran, S. D. (1981). Value orientations in the intimate relationships of gay men. *Journal of Homosexuality* 6 (3): 1–19.

————. (1990). A relationship perspective on homosexuality. In D. P. McWhirter, S. A. Sanders, and J. M. Reinisch (eds.), *Homosexuality/heterosexuality: The Kinsey scale and current research*. New York: Oxford University Press.

Peplau, L. A., and Gordon, S. (1983). The intimate relationships of lesbians and gay men. In E. R. Allgier and N. B. McCormick (eds.), *Changing boundaries: Gender roles and sexual behaviors*. Palo Alto, Calif.: Mayfield.

Peplau, L. A., Padesky, C., and Hamilton, M. (1982). Satisfaction in lesbian relationships. *Journal of Homosexuality* 8 (2): 23–35.

Podbelski, J. J. (1992). Factors involved in marital stability. Unpublished doctoral dissertation, Boston College, Boston, Mass.

Reece, R., and Segrist, A. E. (1982). The association of selected "masculine" sex-role variables with length of relationship in gay male couples. *Journal of Homosexuality* 7 (1): 33–47.

Reibstein, J. (1988). Family therapy and sex role development throughout the life-cycle: A useful concept. *Journal of Family Therapy* 10: 153–66.

Reilly, M. E., and Lynch, J. M. (1990). Power-sharing in lesbian partnerships. *Journal of Homosexuality* 19 (3): 1–30.

Rempel, J. K., Holmes, J. G., and Zanna, M. P. (1985). Trust in close relationships. *Journal of Personality and Social Psychology* 49: 95–112.

Reuman-Hemond, E. (1994). Relationship stability: A qualitative psychological study of long-term lesbian couples. Unpublished doctoral dissertation, Boston College, Boston, Mass.

Rich, A. (1980). Compulsory heterosexuality and lesbian existence. *Signs* 5: 631–60.

Rothblum, E. D. (1988). Introduction: Lesbianism as a model of a positive lifestyle for women. *Women and Therapy* 8: 1–12.

Ryan, C., and Bradford, J. (1993). The national lesbian health care survey: An overview. In L. D. Garnets and D. C. Kimmel (eds.), *Psychological perspectives on lesbian and gay male experiences* (pp. 541–56). New York: Columbia University Press.

Saghir, M. T., and Robins, E. (1973). *Male and female homosexuality: A comprehensive investigation.* Baltimore: Williams and Wilkins.

Scharf, M. (1986). Intimate partners: Patterns in love and marriage. *Atlantic Monthly* 11: 45–93.

Schneider, M. S. (1986). The relationships of cohabiting lesbian and hetero-sexual couples: A comparison. *Psychology of Women Quarterly* 10: 234–39.

Shannon, J. W., and Woods, W. J. (1991). Affirmative psychotherapy for gay men. *Counseling Psychologist* 19 (2): 197–215.

Silverstein, C. (1981). *Man to man: Gay couples in America.* New York: Morrow.

Slater, S. (1995). *The lesbian family life cycle.* New York: Free Press.

Slater, S., and Mencher, J. (1991). The lesbian family life cycle: A contextual approach. *American Journal of Orthopsychiatry* 61: 372–82.

Smith, T. M. (1982). Specific approaches and techniques in the treatment of gay male alcohol abusers. *Journal of Homosexuality* 7 (4): 53–69.

Spanier, G. B., and Lewis, R. A. (1980). Marital quality: A review of the seventies. *Journal of Marriage and the Family* 42: 825–39.

Spanier, G. B., Lewis, R. A., and Cole, C. L. (1975). Marital adjustment over the family life cycle: The issue of curvilinearity. *Journal of Marriage and the Family* 37: 263–75.

Stanley, J. L. (1993). The partnered lesbian and her friends: The impact of friendship on self-esteem and relationship satisfaction. Unpublished doctoral dissertation, University of Pennsylvania, Philadelphia.

Strauss, A., and Corbin, J. (1990). *Basics of qualitative Research.* Newbury Park, Calif.: Sage.

Surrey, J. L. (1984). *Self-in-relation: A theory of women's development.* Work in Progress, no. 13. Wellesley, Mass.: Stone Center Working Paper Series.

———. (1987). *Relationship and empowerment.* Work in Progress, no. 30. Wellesley, Mass.: Stone Center Working Paper Series.

Tannen, D. (1990). *You just don't understand: Women and men in conversation.* New York: William Morrow.

Tanner, D. M. (1978). *The lesbian couple.* Lexington, Mass.: Lexington Books.

Tuller, N. R. (1978). Couples: The hidden segment of the gay world. *Journal of Homosexuality* 3 (4): 331–43.

Walster, E. (1966). Importance of physical attractiveness in dating behavior. *Journal of Personality and Social Psychology* 4: 508–16.

Wamboldt, F. S., and Reiss, D. (1989). Defining a family heritage and a new relationship identity: Two central tasks in the making of a marriage. *Family Process* 28: 317–35.

Weis, C. B., and Dain, R. N. (1979). Ego development and sex attitudes in heterosexual and homosexual men and women. *Archives of Sexual Behavior* 8: 341–56.

White, L. K. (1990). Determinants of divorce: A review of research in the eighties. *Journal of Marriage and the Family* 52: 904–12.

Williams, D. G. (1985). Gender, masculinity-femininity, and emotional intimacy in same-sex friendship. *Sex Roles* 12: 587–600.

Wills, T. A., Weiss, R., and Patterson, G. R. (1974). A behavioral analysis of the determinants of marital satisfaction. *Journal of Consulting and Clinical Psychology* 42: 802–11.

Winfeld, L. (1996). Why can't we marry? *Boston Globe*, Wednesday, 5 June.

Wolfman, B. R. (1984). *Women and their many roles.* Work in Progress, no. 7. Wellesley, Mass.: Stone Center Working Paper Series.

Zevy, L., and Cavallaro, S. A. (1987). Invisibility, fantasy, and intimacy: Princess Charming is not a prince. In Boston Lesbian Psychologies Collective (ed.), *Lesbian psychologies: Explorations and challenges* (pp. 83–94). Urbana: University of Illinois Press.

Index

About the Authors

RICHARD A. MACKEY is Professor at the Graduate School of Social Work, Boston College.

BERNARD A. O'BRIEN is Associate Professor, Department of Counseling, Developmental Psychology and Research Methods, School of Education, Boston College.

EILEEN F. MACKEY has worked in the field of gerontology as an administrator.

ISBN 0-275-95846-9

EAN

9 780275 958466

HARDCOVER BAR CODE